About the Correlation Chart

On the following pages, you will find the Correlation Chart for the All-Star 2 Post-Testing Study Guide. This chart will guide you not only in using the reproducible pages in this book, but also in using the components in the All-Star series to prepare your students for post-testing, and to compile a portfolio to be used for fulfilling competency requirements.

This short but comprehensive guide to using the Correlation Chart will lead you through the chart column by column, allowing you to use this material to best prepare your students for competency and standards testing.

Descriptors

Beginning with the left hand column, you will see a column titled *Descriptor*. This *Descriptor* column contains the competency or standard for which each particular row will provide detailed information. If you are using BEST *Plus,* you will note the descriptor language in italics with a BEST *Plus* indication.

Standards

The next three columns are particular to standards and competencies used across the United States. The second column in the Correlation Chart covers LCP (Literacy Completion Points). Reading down this column, you will see a numbered code indicating which LCP standard a particular *Descriptor* applies to. Continuing to travel to the right, you'll see the following column is titled CASAS (Comprehensive Adult Student Assessment System). Again, reading down this column, you will see a numbered code indicating which CASAS standard a particular *Descriptor* fits. The third column covers BEST *Plus* testing. Reading down this column, you will see a check mark to indicate that the *Descriptor* matches Best *Plus* language testing.

Correlations and Study Guide Pages

The next three columns are titled SB (Student Book), WB (Workbook), and TE (Teacher's Edition). Under each of these columns, you will find page numbers. These page numbers indicate the pages in each component that fulfill a particular competency or standard. Each component page marked in bold face is a reproducible page in this Study Guide. The final column on the right points you to the page in this All-Star 2 Post-Testing Study Guide that covers the *Descriptor* listed in that row.

To the BEST *Plus* Intructor

The All-Star 2 Post-Testing Study Guide correlation chart will point you to pages in the All-Star 2 Student Book, Workbook, and Teacher's Edition that offer exercises and activities covering a wide range of topics and skills to help students prepare for the BEST *Plus.*

On many All-Star 2 Study Guide pages, you will find BEST *Plus* practice questions to use in helping students prepare for the test. In addition, at the back of this Study Guide, you'll find a separate list of practice questions similar to those that may appear on the BEST *Plus* test.

Correlation Chart

Pre-Unit

DESCRIPTOR	LCP	CASAS	BEST+	SB	WB	TE	SG
Identify self and share personal information.	39.01	0.1.4 0.2.1	✓	Pg. 2		Pg. 2	
👂 Ask for clarification and respond appropriately to instructions.	36.04	0.1.6 0.1.2		Pgs. 2, 3		Pgs. 2, 3	

Unit 1: Describing People

DESCRIPTOR	LCP	CASAS	BEST+	SB	WB	TE	SG
Identify self and share personal information. *BEST Plus: State information about country of origin and current residence.*	39.01	0.1.4 0.2.1	✓	Pgs. 12, **13**	Pgs. 2, 3, 4, 5	Pgs. 5, 17, 20	1
Identify required documents related to transportation (driver's license, insurance card, registration, passport).	43.05	1.9.2		Pgs. **4**, 5		Pgs. 5, 20	2
Apply for a driver's license or identification card (eye exam, oral, written, and driving tests).	43.07	1.9.2		Pgs. 4, 5		Pg. 20	
Use appropriate expressions to express feelings and emotions.	39.03	0.1.2 0.1.3	✓	Pg. **8**		Pgs. 11, 12	3
Describe self, family members, and others (physical characteristics and personal traits).	39.02	0.1.4 0.2.1	✓		Pgs. 2, 3, **4, 5**, 6, 7	Pgs. 4, 5, 6, 9, 22	4, 5
👂 Answer incoming telephone calls, take a simple message, leave message, and respond to voice mail messages.	40.02	2.1.7			Pgs. **10**, 11, 14, 15		6
Communicate impressions, likes, dislikes, and acceptance and rejection to invitations.	39.04	0.1.2 0.2.4	✓	Pgs. **10**, **11**, 17	Pgs. 8, 9	Pgs. 11, 12	7, 8
Recognize, state, read, and write statements and questions.	49.01	0.1.2		Pgs. 8, 11, 12, 13, 15, 17		Pgs. 6, 9, 11, 17, 23	
Listen to simple conversations and respond appropriately.	49.02	0.1.2 2.2.1				Pg. 6	
Demonstrate ability to describe a person, place, thing, or event.	49.03		✓	Pg. 8		Pgs. 6, 8, 11	
Write legibly using manuscript and cursive handwriting.	49.11	0.1.2		Pgs. 10, 15		Pg. 20	
Change one grammatical structure of a paragraph to another.	49.15			Pg. 19		Pg. 24	
Read a simple story and utilize context clues for comprehension.	49.16				Pg. **2**		9
Demonstrate ability to use test-taking strategies (circle, bubble in on answer sheet, true/false, and cloze).	49.17	7.4.7		Pgs. 3, 14, 16	Pgs. 14, 15	Pgs. 20, 22	
Use adjectives (demonstrative, descriptive, possessive, comparative/superlative).	50.04		✓	Pgs. 6, 10		Pgs. 8, 9, 11, 12	

Legend:
SB = Student Book   **WB** = Workbook   **TE** = Edition   **SG** = Study Guide   **LCP** = Literacy Completion Point
CASAS = Comprehensive Adult Student Assessment System   **BEST+** = Basic English Skills Test, Updated   👂 = Listening

2 All-Star

Post-Testing Study Guide

Linda Lee ★ Kristin Sherman ★ Stephen Sloan ★
Grace Tanaka ★ Shirley Velasco

 McGraw-Hill

All-Star 2 Post-Testing Study Guide

Published by McGraw-Hill ESL/ELT, a business unit of The McGraw-Hill Companies, Inc. 1221 Avenue of the Americas, New York, NY 10020. Copyright © 2007 by The McGraw-Hill Companies, Inc. All rights reserved. Permission is granted to reproduce these materials as needed for classroom use or for use by individual students. Distribution for sale is prohibited.

ISBN 13: 978-0-07-313813-8
ISBN 10: 0-07-313813-4
1 2 3 4 5 6 7 8 9   QPD/QPD   11 10 09 08 07 06

Editorial director: Erik Gundersen
Developmental editor: Valerie Kelemen
Production manager: Juanita Thompson
Interior designer: Wee Design Group
Cover designer: Wee Design Group
Illustrators: Anna Divito, Andrew Lange, Carlos Sanchis/NETS, Blanche Sims, Chris Winn, Jerry Zimmerman
Photo Credits: All photos courtesy Getty Images Royalty-Free Collection with the exception of the following: page 9 © Bettmann/CORBIS; page 51 © Dennis MacDonald/PhotoEdit; pages 71 and 72 © David Averbach.

The *McGraw-Hill* Companies

Contents

About This Book

Welcome to the All-Star 2 Post-Testing Study Guide. This book provides instructors and administrators with reproducible sample work and information that can be used to help document student readiness for post-testing.

The book has four features:

- All-Star correlation spreadsheet for LCP Level C, BEST *Plus*, and CASAS
- Sample competency documents for portfolio use
- Additional documents to correspond to assessment needs
- BEST *Plus* chart with descriptors and practice questions

The activities from All-Star 2 and the additional documents address the competencies as indicated on the vertical description line of each page. These activities can be used as sample work for student portfolios, and as readiness indicators for post-testing.

Unit 1 (continued)

DESCRIPTOR	LCP	CASAS	BEST+	SB	WB	TE	SG
Use common verbs, contracted forms, and correct spelling in present tense, present continuous, future *(will, going to)*, past tense, present perfect, modals (present, past).	50.02		✓	Pgs. 5, **18, 19**	Pgs. 3, 4, 5, 16, 17	Pgs. 3, 6, 9, 24	10, 11
Use sentence structures (subject, verb, object, affirmative, negative, interrogative).	50.08		✓	Pg. 7		Pg. 24	
Recognize dictionary symbols and produce consonant and vowel sounds.	51.01						12
Produce the beginning, middle, and ending sounds in words including silent letters.	51.02		✓			Pgs. 18, 19	

Unit 2: Going Places

DESCRIPTOR	LCP	CASAS	BEST+	SB	WB	TE	SG
Locate various businesses and government and community agencies in local area (doctor's office, school, hospital, post office, church).	46.01	2.5.3 2.5.5	✓	Pgs. **22**, 23	Pgs. 20, 21	Pgs. 30, 45	13
Interpret traffic and common road signs.	43.01	1.9.1 2.2.2					14
Ask for, clarify, and give simple directions.	43.02	2.2.1		Pgs. 22, 23		Pgs. 33, 34	
Read and understand transportation schedules and road maps (north, south, east, and west).	43.03	1.9.4 2.2.1 2.2.5		Pgs. **26, 27**, 33	Pg. 27	Pgs. 33, 39, 46	15, 16
Identify safe driving practices and consequences of DUI (sobriety test, balance test, jail time, community service).	43.06	1.9.7					17
Simulate making reservations and calculating costs and tips for different kinds of travel.	43.04	1.9.3		Pgs. 24, 25, 28		Pg. 42	
👂 Demonstrate ability to use different types of telephones and telephone options (directory assistance, operator assistance, calling cards, cellular telephone, and Internet access).	40.01	2.1.1		Pg. **31**			18
Locate alphabetical and topical listing information and directory listing in yellow and white pages (restaurants, hospitals, plumbing).	40.04	2.1.1		Pg. 31	Pg. 30	Pg. 45	
Locate various businesses, governmental and community agencies in local area (doctor's office, school, hospital, post office, church, agencies).	46.01	2.5.3 2.5.5	✓	Pgs. 22, 23	Pgs. 20, 21	Pgs. 30, 45	
Write a short note, a friendly letter, and address an envelope, including the return address.	49.12	0.2.3 2.4.1		Pgs. **34, 35**		Pg. 48	19, 20
Write a set of simple directions.	49.14	2.5.4			Pg. 21		
Read a simple story and utilize context clues for comprehension.	49.16				Pgs. 26, 28		

Legend:
SB = Student Book   **WB** = Workbook   **TE** = Edition   **SG** = Study Guide   **LCP** = Literacy Completion Point
CASAS = Comprehensive Adult Student Assessment System   **BEST+** = Basic English Skills Test, Updated   👂 = Listening

Correlation Chart

Unit 2 (continued)

DESCRIPTOR	LCP	CASAS	BEST+	SB	WB	TE	SG
Demonstrate ability to read, and understand basic charts, graphs, maps, tables, and diagrams.	49.09	2.5.4 6.6.5		Pgs. 22, 23, 26, 27, 33	Pgs. 25, 27	Pgs. 33, 34, 39	
Recognize, state, read and write statements and questions.	49.01			Pgs. 20, 22, 24, 26, 28, 31, 32	Pgs. 18, 19, 22, 23, 29	Pgs. 34, 38, 42, 45, 47	
Listen to simple conversations and respond appropriately. *BEST Plus: Describe transportation preferences; describe best ways to travel.*	49.02	0.1.2 2.2.1	✓	Pgs. 22, **28**		Pg. 35	21
Write legibly using manuscript and cursive writing.	49.11			Pg. 35		Pg. 48	
Demonstrate ability to use test-taking strategies (circle, bubble in on answer sheet, true/false, and cloze).	49.17			Pg. 32	Pgs. 20, 21, 30, 31		
Use common verbs, contracted forms, and correct spelling in: present tense, present continuous, future *(will, going to)*, past tense, present perfect, modals (present, past)	50.02		✓	Pg. 21	Pg. 19	Pgs. 31, 47	
Use information questions (who, what, where, when, whose, whom, why, how). *BEST Plus: Understand and respond to information questions.*	50.03	4.6.1	✓	Pg. **23**		Pgs. 33, 35, 36	22
Use adverbs (frequency, time, location).	50.05		✓	Pg. 20		Pg. 31	
Use prepositions.	50.06		✓	Pg. 22		Pg. 33	
Produce sounds of *s* endings: *s, z, iz* (voiced/voiceless).	51.03		✓	Pg. **29**		Pg. 43	23

Unit 3: Dollars and Cents

DESCRIPTOR	LCP	CASAS	BEST+	SB	WB	TE	SG
Demonstrate understanding of Social Security, income tax deductions, W2 and W4 forms. Complete sample W4 form.	35.07	5.4.1		Pgs. 46, 47		Pgs. 67, 68	24
Demonstrate knowledge of operating equipment necessary for home and work.	38.01	4.5.4				Pg. 64	
Count and make change accurately.	42.02	1.1.6		Pgs. **38**, 39, 42, 43	Pgs. 34, 35	Pgs 56, 57, 65, 69	25
Complete a check or money order.	42.03	1.8.2		Pgs. **42**, 43		Pg. 63	26

Unit 3 (continued)

DESCRIPTOR	LCP	CASAS	BEST+	SB	WB	TE	SG
Identify common banking terms and demonstrate ability to use banking services (inquiries, 24-hour teller services, ATM). *BEST Plus: Identify various methods for making purchases and state a preference.*	42.04	1.8.2		Pgs. 36, 37, 40, 41, 44, 45, 48	Pgs. **36, 37,** 38, 39, 40, 41, 42,	Pgs. 53, 56, 59, 62, 64, 73 43, 44, 45	27, 28
Describe the use of an ATM machine and recognize the importance of keeping number codes secure.	42.05	1.8.1		Pgs. **50,** 51		Pg. 71	29
Read and interpret pay stub information.	36.06	4.2.1		Pgs. **46,** 47		Pgs. 67, 68	30
Listen to simple conversations and respond appropriately.	49.02	0.1.2 2.2.1				Pg. 60	
Use common verbs, contracted forms, and correct spelling in present tense, present continuous, future *(will, going to),* past tense, present perfect, modals (present, past).	50.02		✓	Pgs. 37, 39, 50	Pgs. 33, 46	Pgs. 54, 58, 71	
Use information questions (who, what, where, when, whose, whom, why, how). *BEST Plus: Understand and respond to information questions.*	50.03	4.6.1	✓	Pgs. **43,** 51	Pg. 47	Pgs. 63, 72	31
👂 Answer incoming telephone calls, take a simple message, leave message, and respond to voice mail messages.	40.02	2.1.7		Pg. **44**		Pg. 64	32
👂 Demonstrate ability to use different types of telephones and telephone options (directory assistance, operator assistance, calling cards, cellular telephone, and Internet access).	40.01	2.1.1		Pg. 44		Pg. 64	
Demonstrate appropriate communication in 911 emergencies.	40.03	2.1.2					33
Recognize, state, read, and write statements and questions.	49.01	0.1.2		Pgs. 36, 39, 40, 44, 46	Pgs. **38, 39,** 40, 41, 43	Pgs. 53, 56, 59, 62, 64, 67	34, 35
Demonstrate ability to describe a person, place, thing or event.	49.03		✓	Pgs. 40, 42			
Write legibly using manuscript and cursive handwriting.	49.11			Pg. 48		Pgs. 70, 71	
Interpret electric, water, telephone, and credit card bills (account number, current amount due, account balance, due date, past due amount, late payment fee).	40.05	2.1.4		Pgs. 42, 43	Pgs. 42, 43		
Write a short paragraph using correct spacing.	49.13				Pg. 37	Pg. 68	
Change one grammatical structure of a paragraph to another.	49.15			Pg. 51		Pg. 71	
Read a simple story and utilize context clues for comprehension.	49.16				Pg. 42	Pg. 71	
Demonstrate ability to use test-taking strategies (circle, bubble in on answer sheet, true/false and cloze).	49.17			Pg. 48	Pgs. 44, 45		
Produce the beginning, middle, and ending sounds in words including silent letters.	51.02		✓	Pg. **45**		Pg. 56	36

Correlation Chart

Unit 4: Plans and Goals

DESCRIPTOR	LCP	CASAS	BEST+	SB	WB	TE	SG
👂 Demonstrate ability to use different types of telephones and telephone options (directory assistance, operator assistance, calling cards, cellular telephone, and Internet access).	40.01	2.1.1		Pg. 61		Pg. 90	
Answer incoming telephone calls, take a simple message, leave message, and respond to voicemail messages.	40.02	2.1.7				Pg. 90	
Preview and make predictions prior to reading.	49.06					Pg. 86	
Recognize sequential order of events in a paragraph.	49.08			Pgs.59, 66, 67		Pgs. 86, 96	
Demonstrate ability to read and understand basic charts, graphs, maps, tables, and diagrams.	49.09	2.5.4 6.6.5		Pgs. 54, 58, 59, 65, 66, 67	Pg. 49	Pgs. 78, 86, 96	
Plan a schedule of activities on a calendar.	42.01	7.1.4		Pg. 63		Pg. 92	
Read and understand job titles and descriptions.	35.01	4.1.3		Pg. 56		Pg. 83	
Recognize and use basic work-related vocabulary.	35.02	4.1.5 4.1.6	✓	Pgs. **56**, **57**			37
Identify educational and job experience required for specific occupations.	35.03	4.18				Pgs. 80, 81	
Identify the current U.S. President, Vice President, state, and local officials.	46.03	5.5.8		Pgs. 58, 59			38
Recognize the importance of communicating with child's school (meetings, conferences with teachers).	48.01	2.5.5			Pgs. **56**, **57**		39, 40
Recognize compulsory schooling for children 6–16 years of age and the importance of school attendance.	48.02				Pg. 77		
Locate neighborhood school and follow enrollment procedures. *BEST Plus: Locate neighborhood school and describe preferences about schools.*	48.03	2.5.9	✓	Pgs. 61, 62, 63		Pg. 92	41, 42
Recognize the importance of proper child care and acceptable discipline (requirement of food, shelter, hygiene, child care providers).	48.04				Pgs. 56, 57		
Recognize and understand work-related vocabulary for transfers, promotions, and incentives.	37.01			Pgs. 54, 56, 60	Pgs. **58**, **59**	Pg. 83	43, 44
Identify appropriate skills and education necessary for getting a job promotion.	37.02		✓	Pgs. 52, 53, 60	Pgs. 50, 51, 58, 59	Pgs. 77, 78	
Identify appropriate behavior, attire, attitudes, and social interactions for promotion.	37.04	4.4.1 4.4.2			Pgs. 58, 59		
Listen to simple conversations and respond appropriately. *BEST Plus: Describe reasons why people immigrate and choose to become a U.S. citizen.*	49.02	0.1.2 2.2.1	✓	Pgs. **60**, 61			45
Determine the main idea and supporting details in a paragraph.	49.07			Pgs. 58, 59			

Unit 4 (continued)

DESCRIPTOR	LCP	CASAS	BEST+	SB	WB	TE	SG
Recognize, state, read, and write statements and questions.	49.01			Pgs. 54, 58, 61, 63, 64, **66**, 67	Pg. 48	Pgs. 81, 84, 86, 89, 93	46
Demonstrate ability to describe a person, place, thing, or event.	49.03		✓	Pgs. 56, 67		Pg. 83	
Write legibly using manuscript and cursive handwriting.	49.11			Pgs. 56, 64, 67		Pgs. 85, 95, 96	
Write a short paragraph using correct spacing.	49.13			Pg. **67**	Pg. 55	Pg. 87	47
Read a simple story and utilize context clues for comprehension. *BEST Plus: Describe reasons why people immigrate and choose to become a U.S. citizen.*	49.16		✓		Pg. 54	Pg. 86	
Demonstrate ability to use test-taking strategies (circle, bubble in on answer sheet, true/false, and cloze).	49.17	7.4.7		Pg. 64	Pgs. 60, 61	Pg. 93	
Use common verbs, contracted forms, and correct spelling in present tense, present continuous, future *(will, going to)*, past tense, present perfect, modals (present, past).	50.02		✓	Pgs. 53, 55	Pgs. 48, 49, 51, 55	Pgs. 77, 81, 82	
Use adverbs (frequency, time, location).	50.05		✓	Pg. 67			
Produce sounds of past tense endings: *t, d, id,* (voiced/voiceless).	51.04		✓	Pg. **61**		Pgs. 90, 91	48

Unit 5: Smart Shopping

DESCRIPTOR	LCP	CASAS	BEST+	SB	WB	TE	SG
Identify appropriate behavior, attire, attitudes, and social interactions for promotion.	37.04	4.4.1 4.4.2			Pgs. 70, 71		
Communicate impressions, likes, dislikes, and acceptance and rejection to invitations.	39.04	0.1.2 0.2.4	✓	Pgs. 76, 77	Pg.73	Pg. 110	
Demonstrate understanding of comparative shopping.	45.01	1.2.1 1.3.3 1.3.1	✓	Pgs. 68, 70, 72, 73, **74, 75,** 77, 78, 79, 80	Pgs. 66, 67	Pgs. 102, 105, 108, 113, 114	49, 50
Calculate savings when making purchases with coupons.	45.02	1.3.5 1.3.1		Pgs. 72, 73, 78, **79**		Pgs. 105, 106, 107, 113	51
Identify articles of clothing, U.S. sizes, quality, and prices.	45.04	1.1.9	✓	Pgs. **76, 77**			52, 53
👂 Simulate procedures for putting merchandise on layaway.	45.05	1.3.3		Pgs. 78, 79			
Read and discuss simple guarantees, warranties, and procedures to return merchandise.	45.06	1.3.3		Pgs. **78,** 79			54

Legend:
SB = Student Book   **WB** = Workbook   **TE** = Edition   **SG** = Study Guide   **LCP** = Literacy Completion Point
CASAS = Comprehensive Adult Student Assessment System   **BEST+** = Basic English Skills Test, Updated   👂 = Listening

Correlation Chart

Unit 5 (continued)

DESCRIPTOR	LCP	CASAS	BEST+	SB	WB	TE	SG
Ask for and follow directions for locating merchandise in a store (aisle, take the elevator, go left or right, next to the woman's department, at the end of the hall).	45.09	0.1.2 2.2.1 1.3.3		Pgs. 70, 71	Pgs. 64, 65, 74	Pgs. 103, 104	
Calculate savings when items are on sale (percentage, sale price, and regular price).	45.10	1.2.1		Pgs. 74, 75, 80, 81	Pgs. 66, **67**, 75	Pgs. 105, 106	55
Read and discuss various clothing labels (materials, sizes, and washing instructions).	45.11	1.2.1		Pgs. 78, 79			
Use adjectives (demonstrative, descriptive, possessive, comparative/superlative). *BEST Plus: Communicate impressions, likes, dislikes, acceptance, and rejection.*	50.04		✓	Pgs. **69**, 75, 82, 83	Pgs. 63, 76, 77	Pgs. 101, 109, 116	56
Recognize, state, read, and write statements and questions.	49.01			Pgs. 68, 70, 72, 74, 76, 80	Pgs. 68, 69	Pgs. 101, 110, 114	
Demonstrate ability to describe a person, place, thing, or event.	49.03		✓	Pg. 70		Pg. 103	
Demonstrate ability to read and understand basic charts, graphs, maps, tables, and diagrams.	49.09	2.5.4 6.6.5		Pg. 81	Pgs. 65, 67, 74		
Write legibly using manuscript and cursive handwriting.	49.11			Pg. 80		Pg. 115	
Read a simple story and utilize context clues for comprehension.	49.16				Pg. 72	Pg. 108	
Demonstrate ability to use test-taking strategies (circle, bubble in on answer sheet, true/false, and cloze).	49.17	7.4.7		Pg. **80**	Pgs. 74, 75	Pg. 114	57
Use appropriate rhythm and stress in phrases and simple sentences.	51.05		✓	Pg. 77		Pgs. 110, 111	

Unit 6: Food

DESCRIPTOR	LCP	CASAS	BEST+	SB	WB	TE	SG
Use appropriate expressions to express feelings and emotions.	39.03		✓		Pg. 87		
Communicate impressions, likes, dislikes, and acceptance, and rejection to invitations.	39.04	0.1.2 0.2.4	✓		Pgs. 73, 87		
Recognize the importance of healthy eating and maintaining a balanced diet.	41.06	3.5.2	✓	Pgs. 84. 85	Pg. 79		
Read and discuss food labels (ingredients, nutritional information).	45.12	1.2.1		Pgs. 94, 95		Pg. 135	
Read and order from a menu. *BEST Plus: Describe and state opinion about American diet.*	45.03	2.6.4	✓	Pgs. **88**, 89, 92	Pgs. 80, 81, 83, 91	Pgs. 127, 128, 129, 132, 133	58

Legend:
SB = Student Book   **WB** = Workbook   **TE** = Edition   **SG** = Study Guide   **LCP** = Literacy Completion Point
CASAS = Comprehensive Adult Student Assessment System   **BEST+** = Basic English Skills Test, Updated   👂 = Listening

Unit 6 (continued)

DESCRIPTOR	LCP	CASAS	BEST+	SB	WB	TE	SG
Recognize vocabulary and traditions associated with major U.S. holidays and contrast with native customs. *BEST Plus: Describe holidays and customs in one's native country.*	46.04	2.7.1	✓		Pgs. 86, 87		59
Use appropriate rhythm and stress in phrases and simple sentences.	51.05		✓	Pg. **93**		Pgs. 133, 134	60
Write a set of simple directions.	49.14			Pg. **90**		Pg. 131	61
Use information questions (who, what, where, when, whose, whom, why, how) *BEST Plus: Demonstrate understanding and respond to information questions*	50.03	4.6.1	✓	Pgs. 85		Pgs. 122, 123	
Use nouns (count, non-count).	50.07		✓	Pgs. **84, 85,** 91		Pgs. 121, 123, 125, 131, 132	62, 63
Demonstrate ability to read and understand basic charts, graphs, maps, tables, and diagrams.	49.09	2.5.4 6.6.5		Pgs. 84, 85		Pg. 122	
Recognize, state, read, and write statements and questions.	49.01			Pgs. 84, 86, 92, **98, 99**	Pgs. 78, 79, 80, 81, 82, 84, 85, 88	Pgs. 121, 124, 128, 132	64, 65
Demonstrate ability to describe a person, place, thing, or event.	49.03		✓	Pg. 86	Pgs. **88, 89**	Pgs. 125, 126	66, 67
Write legibly using manuscript and cursive handwriting.	49.11					Pgs. 122, 136	
Write a short paragraph using correct spacing.	49.13			Pg. 99	Pg. 87		
Demonstrate ability to use test-taking strategies (circle, bubble in on answer sheet, true/false and cloze).	49.17			Pgs. 84, 94, 96	Pgs. 90, 91	Pgs. 122, 135, 136	
Produce sounds of *s* endings: *s, z, iz* (voiced/voiceless)	51.03		✓			Pg. 127	
Use appropriate rhythm and stress in phrases and simple sentences.	51.05		✓	Pg. **93**		Pgs. 133, 134	

Unit 7: Relationships

DESCRIPTOR	LCP	CASAS	BEST+	SB	WB	TE	SG
Demonstrate understanding of work schedules, time clocks, time sheets, punctuality, and phoning in sick.	36.02	4.2.1 4.4.3			Pgs. 96, 97		
🎧 Demonstrate appropriate communication skills in the work environment (interactions with supervisor and co-workers).	36.05	4.8.1 4.8.2		Pgs. 104, 105	Pgs. 102, **103**	Pg. 148	68
Describe self, family members, and others (physical characteristics and personal traits). *BEST Plus: Describe family members and describe family traditions.*	39.02	0.1.4 0.2.1	✓	Pgs. **100,** 101	Pgs. 93, 99	Pgs. 142, 143	69

Legend:
SB = Student Book   WB = Workbook   TE = Edition   SG = Study Guide   LCP = Literacy Completion Point
CASAS = Comprehensive Adult Student Assessment System   BEST+ = Basic English Skills Test, Updated   🎧 = Listening

Correlation Chart

Unit 7 (continued)

DESCRIPTOR	LCP	CASAS	BEST+	SB	WB	TE	SG
Use appropriate expressions to express feelings and emotions. *BEST Plus: Describe preferences about fun and entertainment.*	39.03		✓	Pgs. 102, 103, **104**, 105, 108, 109		Pgs. 148, 149, 153	70
Communicate impressions, likes, dislikes, and acceptance and rejection to invitations.	39.04	0.1.2 0.2.4	✓	Pgs. 104, 105, 108, 109		Pgs. 148, 149, 153	
Identify procedures for mailing a letter or package (domestic/international), purchasing money orders, and registering mail.	46.02	2.4.2 2.4.6		Pgs. **110, 111**		Pgs. 155, 156	71, 72
Recognize the importance of proper child care and acceptable discipline (requirement of food, shelter, hygiene, child care providers).	48.04	2.5.9 3.5.7			Pgs. **100, 101**	Pg. 161	73, 74
Demonstrate ability to describe a person, place, thing, or event.	49.03		✓	Pg. 102		Pg. 146	
Recognize the meaning of words with common prefixes and suffixes.	49.04			Pg. 109		Pg. 154	
Preview and make predictions prior to reading.	49.06			Pg. 106		Pg. 151	
Use subject, object and possessive pronouns.	50.01		✓	Pg. 114			
Recognize, state, read, and write statements and questions.	49.01		✓	Pgs. 100, 102, 104, 106, 108, 112	Pgs. 92, 93, 96, 98, 99, 100, 101	Pgs. 136, 143, 145, 148, 151, 153, 159	
Demonstrate ability to read and understand basic charts, graphs, maps, tables, and diagrams.	49.09	2.5.4 6.6.5		Pgs. 100, 113	Pgs. **93**, 97	Pg. 142	75
Produce sounds of *s* endings: *s, z, iz* (voiced/voiceless)	51.03		✓			Pg. 143	
Demonstrate ability to use test-taking strategies (circle, bubble in on answer sheet, true/false, and cloze).	49.17	7.4.7		Pgs. 110, 112	Pgs. 99, 103, 104, 105	Pgs. 158, **239**	76
Change one grammatical structure of a paragraph to another.	49.15			Pg. 114			
Use appropriate rhythm and stress in phrases and simple sentences.	51.05		✓	Pg. 109		Pg. 154	
Use nouns (count, non-count).	50.07		✓	Pg. **115**	Pg. 107	Pg. 160	77

Legend:
SB = Student Book   WB = Workbook   TE = Edition   SG = Study Guide   LCP = Literacy Completion Point
CASAS = Comprehensive Adult Student Assessment System   BEST+ = Basic English Skills Test, Updated   👂 = Listening

Unit 8: Health

DESCRIPTOR	LCP	CASAS	BEST+	SB	WB	TE	SG
Identify self and share personal information.	39.01	0.1.4 0.2.1	✓	Pgs. 126, 127		Pg. 179	
Identify body parts and the five senses.	41.01	3.1.1		Pgs. **116, 117**	Pgs. 108, 109	Pgs. 164, 165	78
Describe aches, pains, illnesses, injuries, dental health problems, and follow doctor's instructions. *BEST Plus: Describe methods of treating common illnesses or maladies.*	41.03	3.1.1	✓	Pgs. **118,** 119, 120, 124, 125, 126, 127, 128, 129, 130, 131	Pgs. **110,** 111,112, 113, 120	Pgs. 167, 170, 171, 176, 179, 180, 181, 182	79, 80
Read and interpret medical instructions for prescriptions and over-the-counter drugs. *BEST Plus: Read and interpret information on medicine labels.*	41.04	3.1.1 3.3.2 3.3.3	✓	Pgs. **122,** 123	Pgs. 115 174	Pg. 173	81
Fill out medical history form.	41.07	3.2.1			Pgs. **116, 117**		82, 83
Compare services provided by the health department, hospitals, emergency rooms, and clinics.	41.05	3.1.3			Pgs. **118, 119**	Pgs. 184, 185	84, 85
Demonstrate understanding of safety/warning signs and emergency procedures.	44.01	2.1.2 2.5.1		Pgs. 126, 127		Pgs. 179, 184, 185	
Schedule doctor and dental appointments (first time, routine checkup, follow-up).	41.08	3.1.2 3.1.3		Pg. 124		Pgs. 176, 177	
Demonstrate procedures for first aid (assess individual's condition, procedures to follow after assessment, including calling 911 or administering first aid for minor situations).	41.09	3.1.1 3.4.3 3.4.5		Pgs. **120,** 121, 122, 123, 124, 125	Pgs. 110, 111,112, 113, 118, 119, 120	Pgs. 171, 176, 181, 184	86
Define and use vocabulary for employment (salaries, hours, benefits, sick days, vacation days)	36.01	4.1.6		Pgs. 126, 127			
Ask for clarification and provide feedback to instructions.	36.04			Pg. 125			
Demonstrate ability to describe a person, place, thing, or event.	49.03		✓	Pg. 120		Pgs. 170, 171, 179, 181	
Recognize, state, read, and write statements and questions.	49.01			Pgs. 116, 118, 120, 122, 124,	Pgs. 116, 117 126, 128	Pgs. 165, 170, 173, 177, 179, 180	
Determine the main idea and supporting details in a paragraph.	49.07					Pg. 182	
Recognize sequential order of events in a paragraph.	49.08			Pg. 130	Pg. **113**	Pg. 182	87
Demonstrate ability to read and understand basic charts, graphs, maps, tables, and diagrams.	49.09	2.5.4 6.6.5		Pgs. 117, 126, 127		Pgs. 164, 179	
Write legibly using manuscript and cursive handwriting.	49.11			Pg. 126		Pg. 179	

Legend:
SB = Student Book **WB** = Workbook **TE** = Edition **SG** = Study Guide **LCP** = Literacy Completion Point
CASAS = Comprehensive Adult Student Assessment System **BEST+** = Basic English Skills Test, Updated 👂 = Listening

Correlation Chart

Unit 8 (continued)

DESCRIPTOR	LCP	CASAS	BEST+	SB	WB	TE	SG
Write a short paragraph using correct spacing.	49.13			Pg. 131			
Read a simple story and utilize context clues for comprehension.	49.16				Pg. 113	Pg. 182	
Demonstrate ability to use test-taking strategies (circle, bubble in on answer sheet, true/false, and cloze).	49.17	7.4.7		Pgs. 116, 122, 128	Pgs. 120, 121	Pgs. 165, 174, 180	
Use common verbs, contracted forms, and correct spelling in present tense, present continuous, future *(will, going to)*, past tense, present perfect, modals (present, past).	50.02		✓	Pgs. 119, 125	Pg. 106	Pgs. 168, 176	

Unit 9: Home and Safety

DESCRIPTOR	LCP	CASAS	BEST+	SB	WB	TE	SG
𝒮 Follow generic work rules and safety procedures. Interpret safety signs.	36.03	3.4.2 4.3.1 4.3.2 4.3.4 4.4.3			Pgs. 122, **123**		88
Demonstrate understanding of safety/warning signs and emergency procedures. *BEST Plus: Identify government places in the community and describe public services.*	44.01	2.1.2 2.5.1	✓	Pgs. 136, **138**, 139,	Pgs. 126, 127, 132, 142, 143	Pgs. 193, 197, 201 133	89
Use vocabulary relating to alarm systems (i.e. smoke detectors; fire, house, and car alarms).	44.02		✓	Pgs. **136**, 137		Pg. 194	90
Write legibly using manuscript and cursive handwriting.	49.11		✓	Pgs. 134, 144		Pgs. 192, 203	
Describe various weather conditions and appropriate preparation for weather emergencies.	47.01	2.3.3	✓	Pgs. 138, 139, 140, 141	Pgs. **128**, **129**, 130, 131, 134, 135	Pgs. 196, 197, 199, 200	91, 92
Read various temperatures and compare Fahrenheit to Celsius.	47.02	1.1.5 6.6.4		Pg. **139**	Pg. 129	Pg. 198	93
Describe procedures for basic disposal of trash (regular/large items) and items to be recycled.	47.03	5.7.1					94
Demonstrate knowledge of operating equipment necessary for home and work.	38.01	4.5.4	✓	Pgs. **132**, 133, 134, 136	Pgs. 124, 125,126, 131, 132, 133	Pgs. 187, 188	95
𝒮 Identify various means of locating housing and filling out rental agreements (signs, ads, personal contact, lease, rent, due dates, tenant, and landlord).	45.07	1.4.3 1.4.5 1.4.6	✓				96

Legend:
SB = Student Book   **WB** = Workbook   **TE** = Edition   **SG** = Study Guide   **LCP** = Literacy Completion Point
CASAS = Comprehensive Adult Student Assessment System   **BEST+** = Basic English Skills Test, Updated   𝒮 = Listening

Unit 9 (continued)

DESCRIPTOR	LCP	CASAS	BEST+	SB	WB	TE	SG
Report housing maintenance, repairs, and problems. *BEST Plus: Describe maintenance problems in the home and how to get them repaired.*	45.08	1.4.7	✓	Pgs. **134**, 135, 144, 145	Pgs. 124, 125	Pgs. 191, 202	97
Recognize, state, read, and write statements and questions.	49.01		✓	Pgs. 132, 138, 140, 144, 146	Pg. 133	Pgs. 191, 200, 203, 205	
Demonstrate ability to describe a person, place, thing, or event.	49.03		✓	Pg. 136		Pg. 194	
Recognize the meaning of words with common prefixes and suffixes.	49.04			Pg. 143		Pgs. 187, 201	
Recognize the meaning of compound words.	49.05		✓	Pg. 143			
Recognize sequential order of events in a paragraph.	49.08			Pg. 136		Pg. 194	
Demonstrate ability to read and understand basic charts, graphs, maps, tables, and diagrams.	49.09	2.5.4 6.6.5		Pg. 145	Pg. **127**		98
Write a short paragraph using correct spacing.	49.13			Pg. 138			
Demonstrate ability to use test-taking strategies (circle, bubble in on answer sheet, true/false, and cloze).	49.17	7.4.7		Pg. 144	Pgs. 134, 135	Pgs. 202, 206	
Use subject, object, and possessive pronouns.	50.01		✓			Pg.187	
Use common verbs, contracted forms, and correct spelling in present tense, present continuous, future *(will, going to)*, past tense, present perfect, modals (present, past).	50.02		✓	Pgs. 133, 135, **146**, 147	Pgs. 136, 137	Pgs. 187, 193, 196, 204	99
Produce the beginning, middle, and ending sounds in words including silent letters.	51.02		✓	Pg. 141		Pg. 200	

Unit 10: Work

DESCRIPTOR	LCP	CASAS	BEST+	SB	WB	TE	SG
Read and understand job titles and descriptions.	35.01	4.1.3		Pgs. **148**, 150	Pgs. 138, 139	Pgs. 209, 212	100
Recognize and use basic work-related vocabulary. *BEST Plus: Demonstrate understanding of basic work-related vocabulary.*	35.02	4.1.5 4.1.6	✓	Pgs. 150, **152**		Pgs.209, 210, 212	101
Identify educational and job experience required for specific occupations.	35.03	4.1.8		Pgs. 150, 152	Pgs. 140, 141,150	Pgs. 213, 216	
Use various sources to identify job opportunities and inquire about a job (newspapers, agencies).	35.04	4.1.3		Pgs. 154, 155, **158**		Pgs.215, 219, 221	102
Complete a job application and transfer information to basic resume format.	35.05	4.1.2		Pgs. 162, 163	Pg. 151	Pg. 224.	
Demonstrate appropriate responses to interview questions, proper behavior, and positive image for job interview. *BEST Plus: Demonstrate ability to respond to basic interview questions and recognize acceptable standards of behavior during a job interview.*	36.06	4.1.5 4.2.1	✓	Pgs. 156, 157	Pgs. **140**, **141**, 142, 143	Pg. 219	103

Legend:
SB = Student Book   **WB** = Workbook   **TE** = Edition   **SG** = Study Guide   **LCP** = Literacy Completion Point
CASAS = Comprehensive Adult Student Assessment System   **BEST+** = Basic English Skills Test, Updated   𝔇 = Listening

Correlation Chart

Unit 10 (continued)

DESCRIPTOR	LCP	CASAS	BEST+	SB	WB	TE	SG
Demonstrate understanding of work schedules, time clocks, time sheets, punctuality and phoning in sick.	36.02	4.4.3		Pgs. 156, 157		Pgs. 219, 220	
👂 Follow generic work rules and safety procedures. Interpret safety signs.	36.03	3.4.2 4.3.1 4.3.2 4.3.4 4.4.3		Pgs. 154, 155		Pgs. 217, 218	
Ask for clarification and provide feedback to instructions.	36.04	0.1.2 0.1.6		Pg. 125			
Demonstrate appropriate communication skills in the work environment (interactions with supervisor and co-workers).	36.05	4.8.1 4.8.2		Pgs. 156, 157	Pgs. 140, 141	Pgs. 219, 220	
Identify the importance of job evaluations for promotions and retention.	37.03	4.4.2					104
Identify appropriate behavior, attire, attitudes, and social interactions for promotion.	37.04	4.4.1 4.4.2		Pgs. 154, 155	Pgs. **144,** 145, 148, 149	Pgs. 217, 218	105
Recognize the importance of proper child care and acceptable discipline (requirement of food, shelter, hygiene, child care providers).	48.04	3.5.7			Pgs. 146, 147		
Discuss personal grooming.	41.02	3.5.5 8.1.1			Pg. 144		
Recognize, state, read, and write statements and questions.	49.01			Pgs. 148, 150, 152, 156, 160		Pgs. 209, 213, 215, 219, 222, 226	
Demonstrate ability to describe a person, place, thing, or event.	49.03		✓	Pg. 152		Pg. 215	
Demonstrate ability to read and understand basic charts, graphs, maps, tables, and diagrams.	49.09	2.5.4 6.6.5		Pg. 161			
Write legibly using manuscript and cursive handwriting.	49.11			Pg. 163			
Demonstrate ability to use test-taking strategies (circle, bubble in on answer sheet, true/false, and cloze).	49.17	7.4.7		Pgs. 158, 160	Pgs. 143, 150, 151	Pgs. 221, 222	
Read a simple story and utilize context clues for comprehension.	49.16				Pgs. **148,** 149		106
Use common verbs, contracted forms, and correct spelling in: present tense, present continuous, future "will, going to", past tense, present perfect, modals (present, past)	50.02		✓	Pgs. 149, 151		Pgs. 210, 211, 213	
Use appropriate rhythm and stress in phrases and simple sentences.	51.05		✓	Pg. **157**		Pg. 220	107

Legend:
SB = Student Book   **WB** = Workbook   **TE** = Edition   **SG** = Study Guide   **LCP** = Literacy Completion Point
CASAS = Comprehensive Adult Student Assessment System   **BEST+** = Basic English Skills Test, Updated   👂 = Listening

All-Star 2 Study Guide

Student Name _____   Date _____

Instructor Name _____

---

3 Practice the Conversation: Introducing Yourself 🎧

Listen to the conversation. Then listen and repeat.

A: Hi, my name is Paul. I live on the fifth floor.

B: Hi. Nice to meet you. I'm Cora. I live on the second floor.

A: Nice to meet you, Cora. Do you know Mary? She lives on the second floor too.

B: Yes, I do. She's a good friend of mine.

Practice the conversation with a partner. Use these items.

1 Ted. I work on the second floor.
Meg. I work in the cafeteria.
Meg/works in the cafeteria

2 Sam. I'm in Mr. Reed's class.
Sara. I'm in Ms. Spender's class.
Sara/is in Ms. Spender's class

3 Carl. I'm from Mexico.
Mei. I'm from China.
Mei/is from China

4

Identify self and share personal information. *BEST Plus: State information about country of origin and current residence.*
Student Book page 13. LCP-C 39.01 . . . CASAS 0.1.4, 0.2.1 . . . BEST *Plus*

BEST *Plus:* Where are you from? Where do you live now? How long have you lived in the United States?

Unit 1   **1**

All-Star 2 Study Guide

Student Name _____ **Date** _____

Instructor Name _____

See Student Book pages 4–5.

Identify required documents related to transportation (driver's license, insurance card, registration, passport). Student Book page 4. LCP-C 43.05 . . . CASAS 1.9.2

THINGS TO DO

1 Learn New Words 🎧

Look at the pictures. Listen to the words. Then listen and repeat.

① birth certificate	⑦ sex	⑬ weight
② birthplace	⑧ driver's license	⑭ diploma
③ date of birth	⑨ address	⑮ signature
④ first name	⑩ hair color	⑯ building pass
⑤ middle name	⑪ eye color	⑰ occupation
⑥ last name	⑫ height	

Which words are new to you? Circle them.

2 Check Your Answers

Read the statements. Check (✓) *True, False,* or *I don't know*. Then compare ideas with a partner. Correct the false statements.

	True	False	I don't know
1. Robert's middle name is Manuel.	☑	☐	☐
2. His birthplace is New York.	☐	☐	☐
3. He is now 35 years old.	☐	☐	☐
4. His eyes are brown.	☐	☐	☐
5. He is five feet nine inches tall.	☐	☐	☐
6. Robert is a college student.	☐	☐	☐

3 Interview

Work with a partner. Ask the questions below.

1. What's your first name?
2. What's your last name?
3. What color are your eyes?
4. What's your birthplace?

Write about your partner. Then read your sentences to the class.

EXAMPLE: My partner's name is Gloria Ramirez. Her eyes are brown. Her birthplace is Mexico City.

All-Star 2 Study Guide

Student Name _____   Date _____

Instructor Name _____

See Student Book pages 8–9.

THINGS TO DO

1 Talk About the Picture

Write 5 things about the people in the picture.

> EXAMPLES: Mei has long brown hair.
> Carlos is reading.

Share your ideas with the class.

2 Learn New Words 🎧

Look at the picture. Listen to the words. Then listen and repeat.

① happy	⑤ afraid	⑨ radio	⑬ camera
② relaxed	⑥ bored	⑩ slide	⑭ toy
③ sad	⑦ angry	⑪ swing	⑮ laptop
④ nervous	⑧ tired	⑫ basketball	⑯ cell phone

Which words are new to you? Circle them.

3 Practice the Conversation 🎧

Listen to the conversation. Then listen and repeat.

A: Lynn looks nervous.

B: She is. She is afraid of the dog.

A: That's too bad.

Practice the conversation with a partner. Use these ideas.

1 Amy/ happy	2 Sue/ relaxed	3 Alice/ sad	4 Isabel/ angry	5
likes the slide	has a new book	misses her family	doesn't like the park	
great	nice	too bad	too bad	

★ TRY THIS — Tell about yourself. Check (✓) *often, sometimes, hardly ever,* or *never*. Then compare your answers with a classmate's.

	often	sometimes	hardly ever	never	
I	☐	☐	☐	☐	feel happy.
I	☐	☐	☐	☐	feel nervous.
I	☐	☐	☐	☐	feel _____.

Use appropriate expressions to express feelings and emotions. Student Book page 8. LCP-C 39.03 . . . CASAS 0.1.2, 0.1.3 . . . BEST *Plus*

BEST *Plus:* Look at the picture on page 9 of the Student Book. How do the people feel?

Unit 1   3

All-Star 2 Study Guide

Student Name _____   **Date** _____

Instructor Name _____

Describe self, family members, and others (physical characteristics and personal traits). Workbook page 4.
LCP-C 39.02 . . . CASAS 0.1.4, 0.2.1 . . . BEST *Plus*

A Match the pictures and the descriptions. Write the names on the lines.

Adam

Berta

Cristina

Dan

Eli

1. She has straight gray hair and blue eyes.   _____*Cristina*_____

2. He has a gray beard and a mustache. He is bald.   _____

3. He has short blond hair and green eyes.   _____

4. She has long curly brown hair and brown eyes.   _____

5. He has long straight brown hair and brown eyes.   _____

B Compare Dan and Cristina. Write 2 more things in each place.

Dan only
He is a man.
1.
2.

Dan and Cristina
They don't have beards.
1.
2.

Cristina only
She is a woman.
1.
2.

C Complete the sentences. Write *have*, *has*, *don't have*, or *doesn't have*.

1. Eli _____*doesn't have*_____ brown hair.

2. Dan _____ blond hair.

3. Adam and Cristina _____ gray hair.

4. Berta _____ curly hair.

5. Cristina _____ curly hair.

6. Eli and Cristina _____ brown eyes.

7. Adam and Cristina _____ long hair.

BEST *Plus:* Who are the members of your family? Do you have brothers or sisters? Tell me about your family members.

All-Star 2 Study Guide

Student Name _____   Date _____

Instructor Name _____

D Complete the sentences. Write *is, are, has,* or *have.*

1. Cristina's eyes _____*are*_____ blue.

2. Berta _____ slim.

3. Dan _____ medium weight.

4. Berta _____ brown hair.

5. Berta and Dan _____ long hair.

E Answer the questions about you. Use complete sentences.

1. What color are your eyes?   _____

2. Do you have brown hair?   _____

3. Do you have long or short hair? _____

4. Is your hair curly or straight? _____

5. Are you tall?   _____

F Compare yourself and a classmate. Write 2 things in each place.

My classmate only   Both of us   Me only

1.   1.   1.

2.   2.   2.

Describe self, family members, and others (physical characteristics and personal traits). Workbook page 5. LCP-C 39.02 . . . CASAS 0.1.4, 0.2.1 . . . BEST *Plus*

All-Star 2 Study Guide

Student Name _____   Date _____

Instructor Name _____

Answer incoming telephone calls, take a simple message, leave message, and respond to voice mail messages. Workbook page 10.
LCP-C 40.02 ... CASAS 2.1.7

A Read the message. Check *yes*, *no*, or *I don't know.*

```
TO  Anna
DATE 2/13/05    TIME 10:30 a.m.
        WHILE YOU WERE OUT
Mr. Sergei Andronovich
OF  CTI Bank
PHONE  555-6437
☑ telephoned          ☐ please call
☐ returned your call  ☐ will call back
MESSAGE  He will be 20 minutes
late for the meeting.
```

1. Sergei Andronovich called Patricia.   ☐ yes ☑ no ☐ I don't know.
2. He will be late for a meeting.   ☐ yes ☐ no ☐ I don't know.
3. Anna called Sergei Andronovich.   ☐ yes ☐ no ☐ I don't know.
4. Sergei works with Anna.   ☐ yes ☐ no ☐ I don't know.
5. He called in the morning.   ☐ yes ☐ no ☐ I don't know.
6. Sergei wants Anna to call him back.   ☐ yes ☐ no ☐ I don't know.

B Answer the questions.

1. What date did Sergei call?   _____ 2/13/05 _____
2. What time did he call?   _____
3. Why did Sergei call?   _____
4. What is his telephone number?   _____
5. Where does Mr. Andronovich work?   _____

All-Star 2 Study Guide

Student Name _____   Date _____

Instructor Name _____

See Student Book pages 10–11.

THINGS TO DO

1 Learn New Words 🎧

Look at the pictures. Listen to the words. Then listen and repeat.

① music ③ loud noises ⑤ baseball ⑦ pets
② swimming ④ soccer ⑥ housework ⑧ motorcycles

2 Read and Take Notes 🎧

Listen to the poems. Then read the poems and take notes in the chart.

First name	A. Yuko	B. Paul	C. Abel
Description	brown hair, brown eyes, intelligent		
Likes	music, swimming, Japanese food		
Dislikes	pets, loud noises, the color yellow		
Languages	Japanese, English		
Occupation	student		
Last name	Tanaka		

3 Write

Write a poem about someone you know. Read your poem to the class.

Line 1—the person's first name or given name: _____

Line 2—the person's relation to you: _____

Line 3—three adjectives that describe the person: _____

Line 4—three things the person likes: likes _____

Line 5—three things the person dislikes: dislikes _____

Line 6—languages the person speaks: speaks _____

Line 7—the person's occupation: _____

Line 8—the person's last name or family name: _____

Communicate impressions, likes, dislikes, and acceptance and rejection to invitations. Student Book page 10. LCP-C 39.04 . . . CASAS 0.1.2, 0.2.4. . . BEST *Plus*

All-Star 2 Study Guide

Student Name _____   **Date** _____

Instructor Name _____

See Student Book pages 10–11.

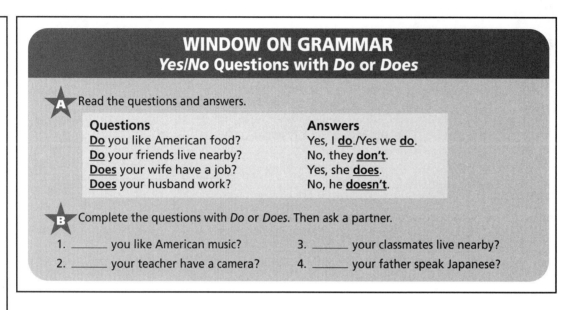

WINDOW ON GRAMMAR
Yes/No Questions with *Do* or *Does*

A Read the questions and answers.

Questions	Answers
Do you like American food?	Yes, I **do**./Yes we **do**.
Do your friends live nearby?	No, they **don't**.
Does your wife have a job?	Yes, she **does**.
Does your husband work?	No, he **doesn't**.

B Complete the questions with *Do* or *Does*. Then ask a partner.

1. _____ you like American music?

2. _____ your teacher have a camera?

3. _____ your classmates live nearby?

4. _____ your father speak Japanese?

Communicate impressions, likes, dislikes, and acceptance and rejection to invitations. Student Book page 11.
LCP-C 39.04 . . . CASAS 0.1.2, 0.2.4 . . . BEST *Plus*

BEST *Plus:* What do you like about living in your neighborhood/this country/this city? What housework do you like better, cooking or washing dishes? What kind of exercise do you like to do? What do you like to do with your family?

All-Star 2 Study Guide for Post-Testing Copyright © McGraw-Hill

All-Star 2 Study Guide

Student Name _____   Date _____

Instructor Name _____

A Complete the sentences.

birth certificate ✓	building pass	diploma	driver's license

1. A _birth certificate_____ is a piece of paper that tells a person's date of birth and birthplace.

2. To drive a car, you need a _____.

3. When you finish high school, you receive a _____.

4. You need a _____ to enter some workplaces.

B Read the story. Match the questions and answers below.

It is 1962:

   John Fitzgerald Kennedy is the 35th President of the United States. He was born on May 29, 1917 in Brookline, Massachusetts. He has blue eyes and brown hair. He lives at 1600 Pennsylvania Avenue in Washington, DC. That's the White House. The president always lives in the White House.

Questions	Answers
1. What is Kennedy's first name?	a. brown
2. What is his address?	b. John
3. What is his birthplace?	c. 5/29/1917
4. What is his date of birth?	d. 1600 Pennsylvania Avenue
5. What is his eye color?	e. Brookline, MA
6. What is his hair color?	f. blue

Read a simple story and utilize context clues for comprehension. Workbook page 2. LCP-C 49.16

All-Star 2 Study Guide

Student Name _____   Date _____

Instructor Name _____

Use common verbs, contracted forms, and correct spelling in present tense, present continuous, future (*will, going to*), past tense, present perfect, modals (present, past). Student Book page 18. LCP-C 50.02 . . . BEST *Plus*

SIMPLE PRESENT STATEMENTS

Regular Verbs

I
You
We   **live** in the U.S.
They   **don't live** in Mexico.

He
She   **lives** in Canada.
It   **doesn't live** in Korea.

Irregular Verbs: Have, Go, Do

have brown hair.
don't have blond hair.
I
You   **go** to school.
We   **don't go** to work.
They   **do** the housework.
don't do the dishes.

has blue eyes.
doesn't have green eyes.
He
She   **goes** to the park.
It   **doesn't go** to school.
does the work.
doesn't do all of it.

---

1 Study the picture of John and Ann. Complete the sentences. Write *have, has, don't have,* or *doesn't have*.

1. John _____ *has* _____ brown hair.

2. Ann _____ brown hair.

3. John _____ curly hair.

4. Ann _____ blond curly hair.

5. John _____ a mustache, but Ann doesn't.

6. They _____ green eyes.

7. John and Ann _____ a new car.

---

2 Read the story about Max and Lisa. Then rewrite the story. Tell about Max.

Max and Lisa

My friends Max and Lisa live in Miami. They own a restaurant there. Max and Lisa like their jobs, but they don't have a lot of free time. They work six days a week. On Monday they don't work. On their day off, they sleep until noon and spend the afternoon at the beach.

Max

My friend Max _____ *lives* _____ in Miami. He _____ a restaurant there. Max _____ his job, but he _____ _____ a lot of free time. He _____ six days a week. On Monday he _____ _____. On his day off, he _____ until noon and _____ the afternoon at the beach.

All-Star 2 Study Guide

Student Name _____   Date _____

Instructor Name _____

Use common verbs, contracted forms, and correct spelling in present tense, present continuous, future (*will, going to*), past tense, present perfect, modals (present, past). Student Book page 19. LCP-C 50.02 . . . BEST *Plus*

YES/NO QUESTIONS WITH THE SIMPLE PRESENT

__Do__	I	need a driver's license?			
__Do__	you	read every day?	__Does__	he	have a building pass?
__Do__	we	like music?	__Does__	she	like motorcycles?
__Do__	they	live in the U.S.?	__Does__	it	live in Texas?

3 Complete the questions with *Do* or *Does*.

1. _____*Do*_____ you have a job?

2. _____ Sam and Dan have beards?

3. _____ you have a cell phone?

4. _____ Tina have short hair?

5. _____ Hector look nervous to you?

6. _____ the president have brown hair?

7. _____ the park have a slide?

8. _____ dogs swim?

9. _____ your friends speak Spanish?

10. _____ your classmates like American food?

4 Unscramble the words to write questions. Remember to capitalize the first word in the sentence.

1. (Victor / camera / does / have / a new / ?)

   Does Victor have a new camera?

2. (like / do / loud / you / music / ?)

   _____

3. (you / do / have / a driver's license / ?)

   _____

4. (you / do / Mr. / Li / know / ?)

   _____

5. (Rick / long / does / hair / have / straight / ?)

   _____

6. (a middle / does / name / the president / have / ?)

   _____

7. (your teacher / curly / does / hair / have / ?)

   _____

All-Star 2 Study Guide

Student Name _____   Date _____

Instructor Name _____

Look at the dictionary page and find the word *ruler.* Answer the questions.

1. What is the first definition of *ruler?* Write it here. _____

2. Say the first consonant in the word *ruler.* How is it pronounced?

3. Say the second consonant in the word *ruler.* How is it pronounced?

rudeness ['rud nəs] *n.* not being polite; bad manners; bad behavior. (No plural form.) □ *The student's rudeness shocked the teacher.*

rug ['rʌg] *n.* a carpet; a thick piece of woven fabric that is used to cover a floor. □ *John vacuumed the rug after he spilled popcorn.*

rugged ['rʌg əd] **1.** *adj.* [of a trail] rough and jagged. (Adv: *ruggedly.*) □ *We had to climb a rugged hill to get to the cabin.* **2.** *adj.* [of something] strong and lasting a long time; [of something] not easily broken. (Adv: *ruggedly.*) □ *The soldier drove the rugged truck across the field of rocks.* **3.** *adj.* [of someone] sturdy and strong. (Adv: *ruggedly.*) □ *The rugged campers lived in the woods for a month.*

ruin ['ru ɪn] **1.** *tv.* to destroy someone or something completely; to make something worthless. □ *David ruined the cake by dropping it on the floor.* **2.** *n.* the remaining part of an old building. (Often plural.) □ *The old house was a nothing but a ruin.* **3.** *n.* a great amount of destruction. (No plural form.) □ *The massive ruin caused by the tornado will be costly to repair.* **4. in ruin** *phr.* in a state of having been destroyed. □ *The crops lay in ruin after the flood.*

ruined ['ru ɪnd] *adj.* destroyed; completely damaged; made worthless. □ *The citizens slowly rebuilt the ruined city.*

rule ['rul] **1.** *n.* a statement that says what one is or is not allowed to do; a regulation. □ *The coach explained the rules of the game.* **2.** *n.* government; the control of someone in authority. (No plural form.) □ *Under the queen's rule, her word was law.* **3.** *tv.* to decide something officially. (The object is a clause with that ⑦.) □ *The court ruled that the law was unfair.* **4.** *tv.* to govern a country or

its people. □ *A tyrant ruled the kingdom for many years.*

ruler ['rul ɚ] **1.** *n.* someone who rules; someone, such as a king or queen, who runs a government. □ *The ruler of the country was only 18 years old.* **2.** *n.* a straight strip of wood, plastic, metal, or other material that has marks on it that show measurement. □ *Susan drew a straight line by tracing the edge of a ruler.*

rumble ['rʌm bəl] **1.** *n.* a low vibrating sound, like the sound of thunder. □ *What is that rumble under the hood of your car?* **2.** *iv.* to make a low vibrating sound, like the sound of thunder. □ *My car engine rumbles loudly when I drive.*

rumor ['rum ɚ] *n.* news about someone or something that may or may not be true; information that is passed from person to person about someone and that may or may not be true. □ *There's a rumor going around that you're moving to Florida.*

rump ['rʌmp] **1.** *n.* the rear part of a person or an animal; the buttocks. □ *The baby fell down on its rump and giggled.* **2.** *n.* meat from the rear part of an animal, used as food. (No plural form. Number is expressed with *rump roast(s).*) □ *The butcher ground up some rump and sold me a pound of it.*

run ['rʌn] **1.** *iv., irreg.* to move quickly in such a way that both feet are off the ground during each stride. (Pt: **ran;** pp: **run.**) □ *Susan ran toward the finish line.* **2.** *iv., irreg.* to work; to be working; to function; to be in operation. □ *The refrigerator isn't running because you haven't plugged it in.* **3.** *iv., irreg.* to extend to a certain length or distance; to reach a certain distance or time. □ *Performances of this opera will run until May 31.* **4.** *iv., irreg.* to flow; [for liquids] to move. □ *The waiter poured the*

All-Star 2 Study Guide

Student Name _____   **Date** _____

Instructor Name _____

See Student Book pages 22–23.

All-Star 2 Study Guide for Post-Testing Copyright © McGraw-Hill

THINGS TO DO

1 Learn New Words 🎧

Listen to the words. Find the places on the map. Then listen and repeat.

1. avenue
2. boulevard
3. on the corner of
4. between
5. next to
6. across from
7. block
8. go north
9. go east
10. go south
11. go west
12. take a right
13. take a left
14. go straight

Which words are new to you? Circle them.

2 Check *True* or *False*

Read the sentences. Look at the map. Check (✓) *True* or *False*. Then correct the false statements.

	True	False
1. The fire station is on Adams Boulevard.	✓	☐
2. The library is next to the drugstore.	☐	☐
3. The medical center is between Central and Green.	☐	☐
4. City Bank is north of the post office.	☐	☐
5. Central Avenue runs east and west.	☐	☐
6. Grove Boulevard runs north and south.	☐	☐

3 Practice the Conversation 🎧

Listen to the conversation. Then listen and repeat.

A: Excuse me. Where's the fire station ?
B: It's on Adams Boulevard between Diamond and Elm .
A: How do I get there from the Medical Center?
B: Just go north on Elm and take a left on Adams .

Practice the conversation with a partner. Ask about these places.

1. community center
2. city bank
3. supermarket
4. restaurant

★ ★

Use the map to write directions. Read them to your classmates.

TRY THIS

EXAMPLE: You are at the corner of Central and Diamond. Go north 4 blocks. Take a left on Grove. Go straight to the second street. What is on the corner?

★ ★

Locate various businesses, and government and community agencies in local area (doctor's office, school, hospital, post office, church). Student Book page 22. LCP-C 46.01 . . . CASAS 2.5.3, 2.5.5 . . . BEST *Plus*

BEST *Plus:* Where do you go to check out books? Where do you usually study? Where do you go when you need to see a doctor? Where do you go shopping?

All-Star 2 Study Guide

Student Name _____   Date _____

Instructor Name _____

Interpret traffic and common road signs. LCP-C 43.01 . . . CASAS 1.9.1, 2.2.2

Match the sign in the first column with the meaning in the second column.
Write the letter in the blank next to the number.

1. _____   A. Traffic signal ahead

2. _____   B. Come to a full stop

3. _____   C. No right turn

4. _____   D. No left turn

5. _____   E. Railroad crossing

6. _____   F. No parking at any time

7. _____   G. Pedestrian crossing

8. _____   H. Do not enter

9. _____   I. One way only

All-Star 2 Study Guide

Student Name _____   Date _____

Instructor Name _____

See Student Book pages 26–27.

THINGS TO DO

1 Check *True* or *False*

Study the map and read the statements below. Check (✓) *True* or *False*.

	True	False
1. Irvine is south of L.A.* (Union Station).	☐	☐
2. Covina is west of L.A. (Union Station).	☐	☐
3. The San Bernardino Line runs north and south.	☐	☐
4. El Monte is directly east of Baldwin Park.	☐	☐
5. Irvine is between Laguna Niguel and Oceanside.	☐	☐

Compare answers with your classmates and correct the false statements.

*Note: L.A. = Los Angeles

2 Read a Train Schedule

Read the train schedule and answer the questions below.

1. It's 7:00 in the morning and Carl is waiting at the Irvine station for a train to L.A. (Union Station). When is the next train?

_____

2. It's 7:30 in the morning and Yun is sitting on train #683. Where is he now? _____

3. How long does it take to get from Irvine to Orange on train #601?

_____

4. How long does it take to get from Oceanside to L.A. (Union Station) on train #603? _____

5. Which train is faster, #603 or #605? _____

3 Write

Write 2 true sentences and 2 false sentences about the map and schedule. Read your sentences to the class. Ask your classmates to identify and correct the false statements.

EXAMPLES: The #683 leaves Oceanside at 5:56.
L.A. County is north of San Diego County.

★ ★

Use the Internet to get schedules for trains near you. Choose a place you want to visit. Print out a schedule of trains from your town or city to this place.

★ ★

Read and understand transportation schedules and road maps (north, south, east, and west). Student Book page 26. LCP-C 43.03 . . . CASAS 1.9.4, 2.2.1, 2.2.5

All-Star 2 Study Guide

Student Name _____   Date _____

Instructor Name _____

WINDOW ON MATH
Measuring Time

| 60 seconds = 1 minute | 60 minutes = 1 hour |

A Complete the sentences.

1. 2 hours = _____ minutes

2. 5 minutes = _____ seconds

3. 120 seconds = _____ minutes

4. 275 minutes = _____ hours and _____ minutes

B Answer the questions.

1. It's 9:30. What time is it twenty minutes later? _____

2. It's 10:40. What time is it a half hour later? _____

3. The train usually leaves at 5:55, but today it is ten minutes late. When will it leave today? _____

All-Star 2 Study Guide

Student Name _____   **Date** _____

Instructor Name _____

Read about drunk driving and answer the questions.

> Do not drink and drive. If you have an accident, you will be charged with DUI, Driving Under the Influence. If you have a drink, get a friend or family member to drive you home. Do not ride with anyone who has been drinking. Here is what can happen if you drink and drive.
>
> - You or your passengers could be injured or killed.
>
> - You could lose your license.
>
> - You may spend time in jail.
>
> - Your insurance may not pay for injuries or damage you cause.

1. DUI means _____

2. You may spend time in jail if you _____

3. Write 3 sentences about why you should not drink and drive.

   _____

   _____

   _____

Identify safe driving practices and consequences of DUI (sobriety test, balance test, jail time, community service). LCP-C 43.06 . . . CASAS 1.9.7

All-Star 2 Study Guide

Student Name _____ **Date** _____

Instructor Name _____

Read the information from the telephone directory.

TELEPHONE DIRECTORY
ALTON-CITY OF

AMBULANCE
Emergency Only.............................. 911

FIRE DEPT. 17 City Plaza
To Report a Fire..............................911
Fire Chief.................................. 555-5940

LIBRARY 2258 N. Main St.
Hours..................................... 555-5849
Information Desk.................................555-3476

MEDICAL CENTER 140 Lincoln Ave.
General Information.............................555-9685

POLICE DEPT. 40 City Plaza
Emergency Only.............................. 911
Citizen Complaint Line........................ 555-9685
Dog Officer.................................. 555-5746
Domestic Violence............................. 555-6958
General Business.............................. 555-6954

POST OFFICES
Washington Square.............................. 555-6845
459 S. Main St. 555-9445
1198 Cross Ave. 555-9347

PUBLIC WORKS DEPT. 594 S. Main St.
Parks and Recreation............................555-5584

SCHOOLS............................... 555-4556

TRANSIT AUTHORITY
Bus Travel................................. 555-9887
Metrolink.................................555-4665

★ ★

TRY THIS Look in your telephone directory. Find the addresses and telephone numbers for these services in your town or city.

AMBULANCE _____

FIRE DEPT. _____

LIBRARY _____

POLICE EMERGENCY _____

POST OFFICE _____

★ ★

All-Star 2 Study Guide

Student Name _____   Date _____

Instructor Name _____

All-Star 2 Study Guide for Post-Testing Copyright © McGraw-Hill

1 Read about the 5 main parts of a letter. Then label the parts of the thank-you letter below.

Main Parts of a Letter	Where	What
1. Heading	in the upper right corner	the writer's address and the date
2. Greeting	on the left side between the heading and the body	*Dear* + name + comma
3. Body	after the greeting	what you want to say in the letter
4. Closing	on the right side below the body	*Sincerely*, *Yours Truly*, etc. + comma
5. Signature	on the right side below the closing	the writer's name in handwriting

1034 Bristol Street
Austin, TX 78722

March 15, 2005 ----- *Heading*

----- Dear Grace,

Thank you so much for the beautiful flowers. They are sitting on my table now as I write this letter. I was very sick. Now I am feeling much better thanks to all of the attention from my friends.

Sincerely, ------- _____

Diedra ------- _____

2 Read about the 3 main parts of an envelope. Then label the parts of the envelope below.

Main Parts of an Envelope	Where	What
1. address	in the middle	the receiver's name and address
2. return address	in the upper left corner	the writer's name and address
3. stamp	in the upper right corner	the postage you buy to send the envelope

Diedra Smith
1034 Bristol Street
Austin, TX 78722

Grace André
526 Broadway Avenue ------------
San Antonio, TX 78209

Write a short note, a friendly letter, and address an envelope, including the return address. Student Book page 34.
LCP-C 49.12 . . . CASAS 0.2.3, 2.4.1

Unit 2   **19**

All-Star 2 Study Guide

Student Name _____   Date _____

Instructor Name _____

3 Write a short thank-you letter to a friend or relative. Include all 5 parts of a letter.

FOCUS ON WRITING: Using Commas

- Use a comma between the name of a city and state or state abbreviation.

  EXAMPLE: Austin, TX

- Use a comma between the day of the month and the year.

  EXAMPLE: March 15, 2005

- Use a comma after the greeting and closing in a letter.

  EXAMPLES: Dear Grace,
  Sincerely,

State	Abbreviation
California	CA
Florida	FL
Illinois	IL
New Jersey	NJ
New York	NY
Texas	TX

4 Address an envelope with your friend or relative's address. Add your return address.

All-Star 2 Study Guide

Student Name _____   Date _____

Instructor Name _____

---

2 Practice the Conversation: Buying a Ticket

Listen to the conversation. Then listen and repeat.

A: I'd like a one-way ticket to Irvine , please.

B: Did you say one-way ?

A: Yes, that's right. When's the next train?

B: 5:15 .

A: 5:50 ?

B: No. 5:15 .

A: Okay. Thanks.

One Way

Chicago
↓
Los Angeles

Round-Trip

Chicago
↕
Los Angeles

Practice the conversation with a partner.
Use these items.

1 a round-trip ticket to Chicago	**2** a one-way ticket to San Diego	**3** a round-trip ticket to Houston	**4**
round-trip/3:13	one-way/2:15	round-trip/4:40	
3:30	2:50	4:14	
3:13	2:15	4:40	

Listen to simple conversations and respond appropriately. *BEST Plus: Describe transportation preferences; describe best ways to travel.*
Student Book page 28. LCP-C 49.02 . . . CASAS 0.1.2, 2.2.1 . . . BEST *Plus*

BEST *Plus:* Do you take a train or bus to school? Do you walk? What are some problems you see with transportation in your city?

All-Star 2 Study Guide

Student Name _____   Date _____

Instructor Name _____

Use information questions (who, what, where, when, whose, whom, why, how). *BEST Plus: Understand and respond to information questions.* Student Book page 23. LCP-C 50.03 . . . CASAS 4.6.1 . . . BEST Plus

WINDOW ON GRAMMAR
Wh- Questions

 Read the questions.

What is he doing at the shopping center?

Who is he talking to?

Where is the police station?

When does the civic center open?

Why is she going to the train station?

How often do you go to the shopping center?

 Complete the questions with *Who, What, Where, When, Why,* or *How often*. Then ask a partner.

1. _____ is he studying at the library?
2. _____ is Scott Street?
3. _____ do you go to a restaurant?
4. _____ does the supermarket close?
5. _____ is eating my sandwich?

All-Star 2 Study Guide for Post-Testing Copyright © McGraw-Hill

All-Star 2 Study Guide

Student Name _____   Date _____

Instructor Name _____

WINDOW ON PRONUNCIATION 🎧
S versus Z

A Listen to the words. Then listen and repeat.

1. place	plays	6. office	offers
2. bus	buzz	7. its	is
3. erase	raise	8. Sue	zoo
4. Miss	Ms.	9. sip	zip
5. police	please	10. rice	rise

B Listen as your partner says one of the words in each pair. Circle the word you hear.

C Choose 5 words from Activity A. Use each word in a sentence.

EXAMPLE: My son likes the zoo.

Produce sounds of *s* endings: *s, z, iz* (voiced/voiceless). Student Book page 29. LCP-C 51.03 . . . BEST *Plus*

All-Star 2 Study Guide

Student Name _____   Date _____

Instructor Name _____

A Read about income tax.

You pay income tax on the money you earn. The government subtracts income tax from your paycheck. Here is how the government figures out how much money to deduct from your paycheck.

- The more money you earn, the more income tax you pay.

- The more dependents you have, the less income tax you pay.

When you fill in a W-4 form, count yourself as one allowance. Count the people you support, your dependents, as one allowance each. Example: You have two children, so you have three total allowances

B Look at the W-4 Form below. Answer the questions. Fill in the form.

1. What should you write next to number 2? _____

2. What should you write next to number 5? _____

3. What should you write next to number 1? _____

4. Do you have to sign the W-4 Form?   yes _____   no _____

Form **W-4**	**Employee's Withholding Allowance Certificate**	OMB No. 1545-0010
Department of the Treasury Internal Revenue Service	▶ Your employer must send a copy of this form to the IRS if: (a) you claim more than 10 allowances or (b) you claim "Exempt" and your wages are normally more than $200 per week.	**2004**

1 Type or print your first name and middle initial	Last name		**2** Your social security number
Home address (number and street or rural route)		**3** ☐ Single ☐ Married ☐ Married, but withhold at higher Single rate. **Note:** If married, but legally separated, or spouse is a nonresident alien, check the "Single" box.	
City or town, state, and ZIP code		**4** If your last name differs from that shown on your social security card, check here. You must call 1-800-772-1213 for a new card. ▶ ☐	

5	Total number of allowances you are claiming (from line **H** above **or** from the applicable worksheet on page 2)	**5**
6	Additional amount, if any, you want withheld from each paycheck	**6** $
7	I claim exemption from withholding for 2004, and I certify that I meet **both** of the following conditions for exemption: ● Last year I had a right to a refund of **all** Federal income tax withheld because I had **no** tax liability **and** ● This year I expect a refund of **all** Federal income tax withheld because I expect to have **no** tax liability. If you meet both conditions, write "Exempt" here . . . . ▶	**7**

Under penalties of perjury, I certify that I am entitled to the number of withholding allowances claimed on this certificate, or I am entitled to claim exempt status.

Employee's signature
(Form is not valid
unless you sign it.) ▶   **Date** ▶

8 Employer's name and address (Employer: Complete lines 8 and 10 only if sending to the IRS.)	**9** Office code (optional)	**10** Employer identification number (EIN)

For Privacy Act and Paperwork Reduction Act Notice, see page 2.   Cat. No. 10220Q   Form **W-4** (2004)

All-Star 2 Study Guide

Student Name _____ Date _____

Instructor Name _____

See Student Book pages 38–39.

THINGS TO DO

1 Learn New Words 🎧

Look at the pictures. Listen to the words. Then listen and repeat.

① toothbrush	⑥ penny (1¢)	⑪ five dollars ($5.00)
② razor	⑦ nickel (5¢)	⑫ ten dollars ($10.00)
③ shaving cream	⑧ dime (10¢)	⑬ twenty dollars ($20.00)
④ shampoo	⑨ quarter (25¢)	⑭ fifty dollars ($50.00)
⑤ toothpaste	⑩ dollar ($1.00)	

2 Write

Complete the sentences with information from the pictures.

1. Dana bought a _toothbrush_ for $3.59. She gave the cashier _$10.00_. He gave her _____ in change.

2. Sam went shopping at the drugstore. He bought a _____ and some _____. He gave the cashier _____. The cashier gave him _____ back.

3. Jim bought some _____ and some _____ for _____. He gave the cashier _____.

3 Practice the Conversation 🎧

Listen to the conversation in a store. Then listen and repeat.

A: The total is $1.25 .

B: Can you change a twenty ?

A: Sure. Your change is $17.75 .

B: Shouldn't that be $18.75 ?

A: Oh, sorry. You're right.

Practice the conversation with a partner. Ask about this money.

1 $5.15	2 $10.50	3 $41.14	4
a ten	a fifty	a fifty	
$4.75	$38.50	$8.56	
$4.85	$39.50	$8.86	

Count and make change accurately. Student Book page 38. LCP-C 42.02 . . . CASAS 1.1.6

All-Star 2 Study Guide

Student Name _____   Date _____

Instructor Name _____

See Student Book pages 42–43.

THINGS TO DO

1 Learn New Words 🎧

Look at the pictures. Listen to the words. Then listen and repeat

① transaction amount   ② balance

2 Read and Take Notes 🎧

Read the personal checks and deposit slips and complete Al's check register on page 43. Then listen and check your work.

3 Answer the Questions

Answer the questions below. Then compare answers with the class.

1. How much money did Al have in his checking account on Sept. 26? _____ *$133.62*

2. How much money did he have on Sept. 30?

   _____

3. How many checks did he write in September?

   _____

4. How much money did he deposit in September?

   _____

★ ★

TRY THIS Complete Al's check #325. Use the information in the check register.

AL MOORE	325
8721 Vista Terrace	
Miami, FL 33109	

DATE_____

PAY TO THE ORDER OF_____ $ [   ]

_____ DOLLARS

BankTwo
Florida

MEMO_____   *Al Moore*

⑆012345678⑆   123⑈456 7⑈ 0324

★ ★

All-Star 2 Study Guide

Student Name _____   Date _____

Instructor Name _____

A Match the pictures and the sentences. Write the letters on the lines. _____

A

B

C

D

1. She is showing a photo ID.   _____C_____

2. He is endorsing a check.   _____

3. She is filling out a deposit slip.   _____

4. He is giving money to the bank teller. _____

B Complete the sentences.

ATM ✓	bank teller	deposit slip	paycheck
savings account	safe-deposit box	withdrawal slip	checkbook

1. The bank is closed today. You can get money at an _____ _ATM_ _____.

2. If you want to take money out of your account, you should fill out a

   _____.

3. I'd like to open a _____, please.

4. Nestor got paid at work today. He needs to deposit his _____.

5. Take this deposit slip to the _____ and she will make sure it

   gets into your account.

Identify common banking terms and demonstrate ability to use banking services (inquiries, 24-hour teller services, ATM). Workbook page 36. LCP-C 42.04 . . . CASAS 1.8.2

All-Star 2 Study Guide

Student Name _____   Date _____

Instructor Name _____

Identify common banking terms and demonstrate ability to use banking services (inquiries, 24-hour teller services, ATM). *BEST Plus:* *Identify various methods for making purchases and state a preference.* Workbook page 37. LCP-C 42.04 . . . CASAS 1.8.2

C Match the questions and answers.

Questions	Answers
1. __c__ Do you have a savings account?	a. No, I have one right here.
2. _____ Where are the withdrawal slips?	b. They're on the counter.
3. _____ What do I need to open a checking account?	c. Not yet. I'd like to open one.
4. _____ How can I use the ATM?	d. You need a photo ID.
5. _____ Do you need a deposit slip?	e. Use your ATM card.

D Answer the questions about you. Write *Yes, I do, No, I don't, Yes, I did* or *No, I didn't.*

1. Do you have a checking account?   _____

2. Did you use an ATM card yesterday?   _____

3. Did you get a bank statement for last month?   _____

4. Do you have a safe-deposit box?   _____

5. Did you get a paycheck for this month?   _____

E Write about your experiences with money. Follow the example below.

I have a checking account, but I don't have a savings account. I pay my rent with a check. I also pay for my groceries with a check. I use cash for toiletries and coffee. Last week I bought a radio. I paid with a credit card. Yesterday I bought a magazine. I paid with cash.

_____

_____

_____

_____

_____

_____

_____

_____

_____

BEST *Plus:* Do you like to go shopping? How do you pay for your purchases (ATM, credit card, check, cash)? Do you think it is a good idea to use a credit card or ATM card?

All-Star 2 Study Guide

Student Name _____ Date _____

Instructor Name _____

SIMPLE PAST STATEMENTS		
Regular Verbs	*Irregular Verbs*	

I
You
He
She
It
We
They
cashed my paycheck.
didn't cash a personal check.

I
You
He
She
It
We
They
went to the park.
didn't go to the bank.

More Irregular Verbs

present	past	present	past
buy	bought	leave	left
come	came	make	made
eat	ate	pay	paid
do	did	put	put
get	got	read	read
give	gave	see	saw
go	went	spend	spent
have	had	write	wrote

1 Complete each sentence below. Use the past tense.

1. I usually cash my paycheck on Friday, but last week I ___*cashed*___ it on Saturday.

2. We usually go to Miami, but last month we _____ to Sarasota instead.

3. She usually gives her son a dollar for lunch, but yesterday she _____ him five dollars.

4. Jan usually goes to work at 8. Yesterday, however, she _____ to work at 9.

5. This year they have a gas stove. Last year they _____ an electric stove.

2 Rewrite the following story. Use the past tense.

John wants to withdraw money from his checking account. He uses the ATM at the grocery store. First, he puts his ATM card into the machine. Then he types in his PIN (personal identification number). The machine asks him how much money he wants. John types in $100.00. Five twenty-dollar bills come out of the machine. The machine asks John if he wants a receipt. John presses the button for "yes". John checks the receipt to make sure it's correct. Then he puts it in his wallet with his $100.00.

John wanted to withdraw money from his checking account.

_____

_____

_____

_____

_____

_____

Describe the use of an ATM machine and recognize the importance of keeping number codes secure. Student Book page 50. LCP-C 42.05 . . . CASAS 1.8.1

Unit 3   **29**

All-Star 2 Study Guide

Student Name _____   Date _____

Instructor Name _____

Read and interpret pay stub information. Student Book page 46. LCP-C 36.06 . . . CASAS 4.2.1

1 Learn New Words

Guess the meanings of the underlined words. Circle the best answer or definition.

1. Andy is an <u>employee</u> at Bank Two. He works as a
   bank teller. An employee is a _____.
   A. customer   B. worker   C. student

2. Andy's <u>salary</u> from Bank Two is $800.00 a week. His
   salary is his _____.
   A. rent   B. utilities   C. pay

3. Andy earns $800.00 a week, but Bank Two <u>deducts</u>
   $120.00 for taxes. He gets a paycheck for $680.00
   every week. Another word for *deducts* is _____.
   A. adds   B. subtracts   C. equals

2 Answer the Questions

Read the pay stub. Answer the questions below.

BankTwo   Employee name: **Andy Kalish**   Period beginning: 02/01/05
                                                Period ending: 02/15/05

SOCIAL SECURITY NUMBER: **928-62-5555**

Earnings	Hours Worked This Pay Period	Earnings This Pay Period	Earnings Year to Date
$20.00/hour	80	$1,600.00	$4,800.00
Federal taxes deducted		− $ 240.00	− $ 720.00
State taxes deducted		− $ 80.00	− $ 240.00
FICA		− $ 30.00	− $ 90.00
Health insurance		− $ 15.00	− $ 45.00
Check amount		$1,235.00	$3,705.00

FICA is a tax that is used to pay for retirement benefits, or Social Security.

1. What is Andy's pay per hour? _His pay is $20.00 per hour._____

2. How many hours did he work in this pay period? _____

3. How long is this pay period? _____

4. What was the amount of his paycheck this pay period? _____

5. How much was deducted from this check for health insurance? _____

All-Star 2 Study Guide for Post-Testing Copyright © McGraw-Hill

All-Star 2 Study Guide

Student Name _____   Date _____

Instructor Name _____

WINDOW ON GRAMMAR
Wh- Questions + Past Tense

 Read the questions. Then ask a partner.

Who did you **talk** to yesterday?

What did you **do** in the morning?

Where did you **go** yesterday?

When did you **get** up?

Why did you **open** a checking account?

How much money **did** you **spend**?

B Write 6 new questions. Ask a partner.

1. Who did . . . ?   3. What did . . . ?   5. Where did . . . ?
2. When did . . . ?   4. Why did . . . ?   6. How much . . . ?

Use information questions (who, what, where, when, whose, whom, why, how). *BEST Plus: Understand and respond to information questions.* Student Book page 43. LCP-C 50.03 . . . CASAS 4.6.1 . . . BEST *Plus*

All-Star 2 Study Guide

Student Name _____   Date _____

Instructor Name _____

Answer incoming telephone calls, take a simple message, leave message, and respond to voice mail messages. Student Book page 44.
LCP-C 40.02 . . . CASAS 2.1.7

---

1 Listen and Write: Listening to an Automated System 🎧

Listen and write the missing words. Then listen and check your answers.

Thank you for calling Horizon Bank. For existing account information, press _____. For all other services, press _____. To speak to a customer service specialist at any time, press _____.

For checking accounts, press _____. For savings, press _____. For credit cards, press _____.

Please enter your checking account number followed by the # sign. For personal accounts, please enter the last four digits of your social security number followed by the # sign.

Your available _____ is _____.

All-Star 2 Study Guide

Student Name _____   Date _____

Instructor Name _____

A Read the conversation about a 911 emergency.

Jeremy: What's the problem?
Louise: I have a terrible headache. Should I call 911?
Jeremy: No. That's not an emergency.

B Should you call 911? Check yes or no.

Someone is bleeding a lot.	_____ yes	_____ no
Someone has a terrible cough.	_____ yes	_____ no
Someone drank detergent.	_____ yes	_____ no
Someone has a sore throat.	_____ yes	_____ no
Someone was hit by a bus.	_____ yes	_____ no
Someone is choking.	_____ yes	_____ no
Someone has a horrible headache.	_____ yes	_____ no
Someone has a runny nose.	_____ yes	_____ no
Someone isn't breathing.	_____ yes	_____ no
Someone is having a heart attack.	_____ yes	_____ no

C Write a conversation about a phone call to 911.

A: 911. What's your emergency?

B: _____

A: Where are you located?

B: _____

A: We're sending someone right now.

Demonstrate appropriate communication in 911 emergencies. LCP-C 40.03 . . . CASAS 2.1.2

All-Star 2 Study Guide

Student Name _____   Date _____

Instructor Name _____

A Read the information. Check *yes* or *no* to the questions below.

Bank of Westville

Contact Us • Help

BANK OF WESTVILLE

SEARCH

| ABOUT THE BANK | ACCOUNTS | BUSINESSES | LOCATIONS |

Be Smart About Your Checking Account

1. If you don't have money in your checking account, don't write checks.
2. Balance your checkbook often. Include ATM withdrawals on your check register.
3. Check your monthly bank statement every month.
4. If two people share one account, have one person keep track of the balance. Keep receipts in a safe place.
5. Use cash for small purchases. The fewer checks you write, the easier it is to keep track.
6. Have your paycheck deposited directly to your account. This way you avoid losing your check.
7. Learn about your account. You should know what fees the bank charges for checks and deduct those fees on your check register.

---

1. It's okay to write checks when there is no money in your account.
   ❏ yes   ☑ no

2. You should check your monthly bank statement.
   ❏ yes   ❏ no

3. You should use cash when you are buying things that don't cost much money.
   ❏ yes   ❏ no

4. You should balance your checkbook often.
   ❏ yes   ❏ no

5. You don't need to write down ATM withdrawals in your check register.
   ❏ yes   ❏ no

Student Name _____   Date _____

Instructor Name _____

B Answer the questions.

1. What should you know about your account?   *wh-* **questions**

   You should know what fees the bank charges.

2. When should you check your monthly bank statement?

   _____

3. Where should you write your ATM withdrawals?

   _____

4. Why should you use cash for small purchases?

   _____

C Circle the correct answer.

1. What did you buy?   *wh-* **questions + past tense**
   A. a toothbrush   B. last night

2. Where did you write the amount?
   A. to balance my checkbook   B. in my check register

3. Who did you write the check to?
   A. Sim's Drugs   B. I did.

4. Why did you use a check?
   A. in the store   B. I didn't have cash.

5. How much did you pay for it?
   A. every month   B. $1.89

D Answer the questions about you. Write complete sentences.

1. What did you buy last week?

   _____

2. How did you pay for your purchases?

   _____

3. When did you balance your checkbook last?

   _____

All-Star 2 Study Guide

Student Name _____   Date _____

Instructor Name _____

WINDOW ON PRONUNCIATION 🎧
Ng versus *Nk*

A Listen to the words. Then listen and repeat.

bank	bang	saving	sink	think
thank	thing	sing	nothing	checking
ink	drink	long	wondering	young

B Listen to each pair of questions below. Then listen and repeat.

Questions	Answers
1. What is that bank? What is that bang?	a. First National Bank. b. Something fell in the kitchen.
2. Do you have a sink? Do you have to sing?	a. Yes, in the bathroom. b. No, I can tell a story.
3. Now think. What do you want? Nothing. What do you want?	a. I can't. I'm too tired. b. I don't want anything either.

C Now listen again. You will hear one question from each pair in Activity B. Circle the correct answer.

All-Star 2 Study Guide

Student Name _____   Date _____

Instructor Name _____

See Student Book pages 56–57.

Recognize and use basic work-related vocabulary. Student Book page 56. LCP-C 35.02 . . . CASAS 4.1.5, 4.1.6 . . . BEST *Plus*

THINGS TO DO

1 Learn New Words

Look at the picture. Listen to the words. Then listen and repeat.

1. office manager
2. office worker
3. designer
4. bookkeeper
5. salesperson
6. supervisor
7. mechanic
8. late
9. on time
10. organized
11. disorganized
12. good with people
13. hardworking
14. lazy
15. bad attitude
16. good attitude

Which words are new to you? Circle them.

2 Talk About the Picture

Write 5 sentences about the picture. Then share ideas with the class.

EXAMPLE: I think the office manager is angry.

3 Practice the Conversation

Listen to the conversation. Then listen and repeat.

A: Who's going to get the job as the new bookkeeper ?

B: I think Jon will. He's organized .

A: Yes, and he is always on time .

1 sales manager	2 supervisor	3 salesperson
Ben/hardworking	Tim/never late	Ken/ good with people
has a good attitude	is good with people	is always organized

4 Find Someone Who

Talk to your classmates. Find someone who answers yes to your question. Write the person's name in the chart.

Find someone who _____.	Person's Name
1. wants to supervise others	_____
2. is very organized	_____
3. is usually on time	_____
4. wants to work in an office	_____

All-Star 2 Study Guide

Student Name _____   Date _____

Instructor Name _____

Identify the current U.S. President, Vice President, state, and local officials. LCP-C 46.03 . . . CASAS 5.5.8

Answer the questions.

1. Who is the President of the United States? _____

2. Who is the Vice President of the United States? _____

3. Who is the Governor of your state? _____

4. Name one Senator from your state. _____

5. Name one representative from your state. _____

6. Who is the mayor of your city or town? _____

7. Who is the principal of your school? _____

All-Star 2 Study Guide for Post-Testing Copyright © McGraw-Hill

All-Star 2 Study Guide

Student Name _____   Date _____

Instructor Name _____

A Check the box if you agree.

☐ Parents should read to their children.

☐ Parents should spend time with their children.

☐ Learning is important for everyone in the family.

☐ Parents should help with homework.

☐ All adult family members should be involved in children's school.

B Read the information. Check *True* or *False* to the questions that follow on page 57.

EDUCATIONAL DATABASE.COM

Search our online database!

[_____]

[GO]

Help Your Child Succeed In School!

Encourage your child to read.
- Start early, when your child is still a baby.
- Keep books, magazines, and newspapers in the house.
- Show that you like to read. Read as much as you can.
- Get your child help if she or he has a problem with reading.

Talk to your child.
- Talk about school and things you see around you.
- When you go shopping, talk about prices.
- When you are cooking, talk about food and recipes.
- When you watch TV, talk about the programs.
- Pay attention when your child is talking to you.

Help with homework.
- Provide a good place to study.
- Schedule time for homework.
- Turn off the TV and other distractions.
- Tell your child when he or she does a good job.
- Don't worry if your English isn't perfect, you are not doing the homework.

Limit television and video games.
- Don't let your child spend too much time in front of the TV or video screen.
- Watch what your child watches.

Use the library.
- Bring your child to the library often.
- Get your child a library card.
- Ask about special programs at the library.
- Teach your child responsible use of the Internet.

Encourage your child to be responsible.

Recognize the importance of communicating with child's school (meetings, conferences with teachers). Workbook page 56.
LCP-C 48.01 . . . CASAS 2.5.5

All-Star 2 Study Guide

Student Name _____   Date _____

Instructor Name _____

See Workbook page 56. Read the information and answer the questions.

	True	False
1. You don't need to read to babies because they are too young to understand.	☐	☐
2. You shouldn't let your children watch too much TV. When they do watch, you should watch with them.	☐	☐
3. Children should get their own library cards.	☐	☐
4. If your children don't understand their homework, you should do it for them.	☐	☐
5. If your English isn't very good, you can't help with homework.	☐	☐

C Answer the questions.

1. What are 3 things you can talk about with your child?

   _____

2. What are 3 things you should have in your house to read?

   _____

3. How can you help with homework?

   _____

★ ★

TAKE IT OUTSIDE: Interview a family member, friend, or coworker. Write the answers in the chart.

NUMBER OF CHILDREN	HOW DO YOU HELP YOUR CHILDREN WITH READING?	HOW DO YOU HELP YOUR CHILDREN WITH HOMEWORK?

★ ★

TAKE IT ONLINE: Use the Internet to find information on "how to help children succeed in school." Write 2 new ideas you learn.

1. _____

2. _____

All-Star 2 Study Guide

Student Name _____   Date _____

Instructor Name _____

Read the information. Check *True* or *False*.

Dale City Public Schools
Registration Requirements

Determining the School

Students must register at their neighborhood school. Parents can call 688-721-1234 to find out the name and address of their child's school.

Documents Required

- An original birth certificate
- Proof of immunization
- Proof of Tuberculosis screening

Parents must fill out a Home Language Survey. See the sample of the Language Questionnaire.

Answer the following questions.

1. Parents must register their children at the neighborhood school.   True_____   False_____

2. Three documents are required for registration.   True_____   False_____

3. Parents must fill out a Home Language Survey.   True_____   False_____

BEST *Plus:* Where do children in your area go to school? Do you like the schools in your city/neighborhood?

Unit 4   **41**

All-Star 2 Study Guide

Student Name _____   Date _____

Instructor Name _____

Read the information and answer the questions.

Miami City Adult School

Registration begins: Monday, March 14 in the Main Office. See Dr. Diaz.

Registration hours:
Monday, Wednesday, Friday	10 A.M. – 8:30 P.M.
Tuesday, Thursday	Noon – 8 P.M.
Saturday	8 – 11 A.M.

Orientation:
Monday thru Thursday	9 A.M. – 1 P.M.
Friday	5 – 9 P.M.

Classes begin: Monday, March 21

General Information

You must register in person.

You must have a photo ID and Social Security card.

If you want to take English classes, you must take a placement test.

There is a $15 registration fee.

1. When does registration begin? _____

2. What are the registration hours on Tuesday and Thursday? _____

3. How much is the registration fee? _____

4 When do classes begin? _____

5. What do students have to bring to registration? _____

All-Star 2 Study Guide

Student Name _____   Date _____

Instructor Name _____

Recognize and understand work-related vocabulary for transfers, promotions, and incentives. Workbook page 58. LCP-C 37.01

A Look at the article. Check the things you think will be in the article.

- ❑ ways to get a promotion
- ❑ how to make plans
- ❑ the qualities you need for a better job
- ❑ the classes you should take
- ❑ how to fill out an application
- ❑ what to wear to an interview
- ❑ the importance of skills and achievements

B Read the article. Check your answers in Activity A.

HOW TO GET A PROMOTION

Do you want a new job or promotion? Follow the steps below and you may get a better position.

1. **Make a plan:** You need to have a plan. What job or position do you want? When do you plan to get the position? What skills or training do you need for the new position?

2. **Do more:** Start doing more work in your job now. Show your supervisor that you are hardworking. Always come to work and meetings on time, and call when you are sick.

3. **Learn more:** A promotion or new job often needs more training or education. Find out what classes or training you can take.

4. **Have a good attitude:** Don't think of your work as just a job. Be pleasant, accept reponsibility, and work hard.

5. **Look the part:** You should dress, speak, and act like the employee in the position you want. Dress neatly, speak politely, and act appropriately.

6. **List your skills and achievements:** Think about your skills and achievements. Can you do anything special? Did you do good work in your last job?

7. **Tell your supervisor:** Your supervisor can help you get a promotion. Tell your supervisor you would like a new position. Ask questions about the position. Find out what you need to do.

All-Star 2 Study Guide

Student Name _____ **Date** _____

Instructor Name _____

See Workbook page 58.

Recognize and understand work-related vocabulary for transfers, promotions, and incentives. Workbook page 59. LCP-C 37.01

C Read the article again. Complete the sentences.

1. If you want a promotion, you should tell _____.

2. You need to show that you are _____.

3. Always come to work _____.

4. If you are sick, you should _____.

5. Find out _____ to get a promotion.

D Complete the sentences about you.

1. If I want to get a promotion, I should learn _____.

2. If I want to get a better job, I should be _____ and

   _____.

3. If I want my supervisor to help me, I should _____.

★ ★

TAKE IT OUTSIDE: Interview a family member, friend, or coworker. Write the answers.

1. Did you get a raise or a promotion in your job? _____

2. Why? _____

3. What do you think someone should do to get a promotion?

   _____

   _____

★ ★

All-Star 2 Study Guide for Post-Testing Copyright © McGraw-Hill

All-Star 2 Study Guide

Student Name _____   Date _____

Instructor Name _____

---

2 Practice the Conversation: Asking for Advice 🎧

Listen to the conversation. Then listen and repeat.

A: You look happy. What's up?

B: I just got a raise .

A: That's great. I want to get a raise , too. How did you do it?

B: I worked hard and was always on time .

A: That's good advice.

Practice the conversation with a partner. Use these ideas.

1
got a promotion
get a promotion
went back to school

2
retired
retire
worked hard and saved money

3
bought a house
buy a house
saved money for ten years

4
started my own business
start my own business
took some business classes

5
💡

Listen to simple conversations and respond appropriately. *BEST Plus: Describe reasons why people immigrate and choose to become a U.S. citizen.* Student Book page 60. LCP-C 49.02 . . . CASAS 0.1.2, 2.2.1 . . . *BEST Plus*

BEST *Plus:* Why did you come to this country? Why do people immigrate to another country? Is it important for immigrants to become citizens?

Unit 4   45

All-Star 2 Study Guide

Student Name _____   Date _____

Instructor Name _____

1 Read the story. Number the pictures from first (1) to last (6). Then complete the timeline.

AN IMPORTANT EVENT IN MY LIFE

by James St. Fleur

An important event in my life was on December 22, 1990. That's when my second son was born in Miami. I didn't watch when my older children were born. In Haiti, the father can't go into the hospital delivery room.

My wife started labor very early in the morning. I drove my wife to the hospital and the nurses put her in a room. Over the next few hours, they checked on her several times. Finally, they asked me to put on a hospital gown, and they took my wife and me to the delivery room. In less than an hour the baby came. The doctor gave me a pair of scissors and I cut the baby's umbilical cord. Then I held my son for the first time. I was very excited to see how my baby came into the world.

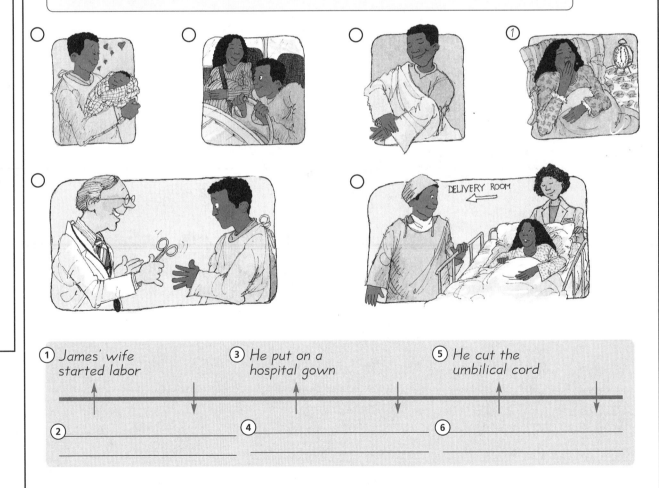

Timeline:

① James' wife started labor   ③ He put on a hospital gown   ⑤ He cut the umbilical cord

② _____   ④ _____   ⑥ _____

All-Star 2 Study Guide

Student Name _____   **Date** _____

Instructor Name _____

See Student Book pages 66–67.

3 Choose an important event in your life. Make a timeline with information about the event. Then write about the event. Use time words and phrases in your story.

→ _____

_____

_____

_____

_____

_____

_____

_____

_____

_____

_____

_____

_____

_____

Write a short paragraph using correct spacing. Student Book page 67. LCP-C 49.13

All-Star 2 Study Guide

Student Name _____   Date _____

Instructor Name _____

WINDOW ON PRONUNCIATION
Past Tense Endings

 Listen to the words. Then listen and repeat.

1. married	4. relaxed	7. cashed	10. studied	13. divorced
2. wanted	5. liked	8. deposited	11. graduated	14. used
3. moved	6. helped	9. immigrated	12. learned	15. promoted

 Write the words in the correct place in the chart.

Ending sounds like *t*	Ending sounds like *d*	Ending sounds like *id*
1. *relaxed*	1. *married*	1. *wanted*
2.	2.	2.
3.	3.	3.
4.	4.	4.
5.	5.	5.

 Complete the rules.

1. If the word ends in a *voiceless* consonant sound (*ck, k, f, p, ch, sh, s, x*), the past tense ending (*ed*) sounds like _____.
2. If the word ends in a *voiced* consonant sound (*b, g, j, m, n, r, z*) or a vowel sound, the past tense ending (*ed*) sounds like _____.
3. If the word ends in a *t* or *d* sound, the past tense ending (*ed*) sounds like _____.

D Work with a partner. Ask and answer the questions. Use complete sentences.

1. What did you like to do when you were a child?
2. What kind of job did you want when you were young?
3. What was the best thing you learned in school as a child?

All-Star 2 Study Guide

Student Name _____   Date _____

Instructor Name _____

See Student Book pages 74–75.

Demonstrate understanding of comparative shopping. Student Book page 74. LCP-C 45.01 . . . CASAS 1.2.1, 1.3.3, 1.3.1 . . . BEST *Plus*

THINGS TO DO

1 Preview

Scan the article. Which of the things below can you learn from it? Check (✓) your answers.

☐ when things are on sale

☐ which stores are cheaper

☐ how much appliances cost

☐ what you should buy in the winter

2 Read and Take Notes

Read the article and take notes in the chart below.

ITEM	THE BEST TIME TO BUY
summer clothes	*in September*
outdoor furniture	
fall clothes	
stereos	
spring clothes	
sheets and towels	
televisions	

3 Write

Look in a newspaper for information about sales in your area. Then write about the sales that interest you.

EXAMPLE: It's February now, and a lot of things are on sale. At Leblanc's True Value Hardware store, everything is 10–70% off. At Fortunes, winter clothes are on sale. On February 6 and 7, you can get an extra 20% off already marked-down clothes.

★ ★

TRY THIS   Use the Internet to shop for sales. Go online and look for a store you know. Find the sale section on the store's web site. Choose one item. Tell your classmates the original price and the sale price.

★ ★

BEST *Plus:* Are clothes or furniture in the United States cheap or expensive? Do you use coupons when you shop?

Unit 5   **49**

All-Star 2 Study Guide

Student Name _____   **Date** _____

Instructor Name _____

See Student Book pages 74–75.

Demonstrate understanding of comparative shopping. Student Book page 75. LCP-C 45.01 … CASAS 1.2.1, 1.3.3, 1.3.1 … BEST *Plus*

WINDOW ON GRAMMAR
Superlatives

A Read the sentences.

<u>**The best**</u> time to buy sheets is in January.
<u>**The worst**</u> time to buy garden supplies is in the spring.

ADJECTIVE	COMPARATIVE	SUPERLATIVE
good →	better →	the best
bad →	worse →	the worst
cheap →	cheaper →	the cheapest
expensive →	more expensive →	the most expensive

B Complete the sentences.

1. Fall clothes are the _____ in January.

2. September is the _____ time to buy plants.

3. April is a _____ time to buy spring clothes, but August is the _____ time.

All-Star 2 Study Guide for Post-Testing Copyright © McGraw-Hill

All-Star 2 Study Guide

Student Name _____   Date _____

Instructor Name _____

Read the shopping tips.

Tips From Smart Shoppers

Tip #1 Use Store Coupons

You can save money by cutting coupons from newspapers and store flyers. Just give the coupons to the cashier when you make your purchase, and you'll get a discount. Keep these things in mind when you use coupons:

- Check the date on the coupon. Most coupons are valid, or good, for a short period of time.
- Stores use coupons to get you to buy something you don't really need.

STOREWIDE BONUS COUPON
EXTRA **15%** OFF
VALID FRIDAY AND SATURDAY
JUNE 6 & 7
MAY'S DEPARTMENT STORE
3993044 37756
NO DISCOUNT on jewelry or cosmetics.

Tip #2 Use Layaway

Many stores have layaway plans. You make a deposit or down payment, and you have a certain amount of time to complete your payment. The store keeps the item until you pay in full. Usually there is no extra fee or service charge.

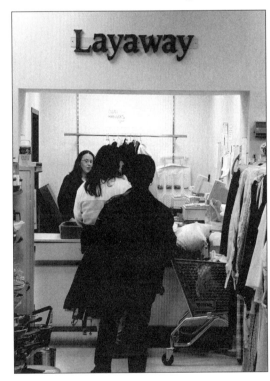

Tip #3 Read the Warranty

A warranty or guarantee tells what a company will do if you have a problem with something you buy. It's especially important to read the warranty before you buy something expensive. You should also save the warranty and any packaging your purchase came in.

SHARK® Washing Machine Warranty

Full One-Year Warranty

For one (1) year from the date of original retail purchase, any part that fails in normal home use will be repaired or replaced free of charge.

To Receive Warranty Service

Call Shark Customer Service toll-free at 1-555-456-4566. You will need the model and serial numbers of your appliance, the name and address of the dealer, and the date of purchase.

All-Star 2 Study Guide

Student Name _____   Date _____

Instructor Name _____

Identify articles of clothing, U.S. sizes, quality, and prices. Student Book page 76. LCP-C 45.04 . . . CASAS 1.1.9 . . . BEST *Plus*

1 Practice the Conversation: Exchanging Something 🎧

Listen to the conversation. Then listen and repeat.

A: Can I help you?

B: Yes. I want to return this jacket .

A: Okay. Was there something wrong with it?

B: Yes. It's too tight .

A: Do you want to exchange it for a looser one ?

B: Yes, I do.

A: Okay. I'll be right with you.

Practice the conversation with a partner. Use these items.

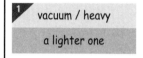
1 vacuum / heavy
a lighter one

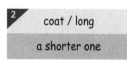
2 coat / long
a shorter one

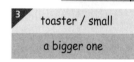
3 toaster / small
a bigger one

4 💡

2 Practice the Conversation: Asking for a Refund 🎧

Listen to the conversation. Then listen and repeat.

A: Can I help you?

B: Yes, I want to return these toys . They're just too noisy .

A: Do you want some quieter ones?

B: No, thank you. I just want a refund.

A: Do you have your receipt?

B: Yes, I have it right here.

Practice the conversation with a partner. Use these items.

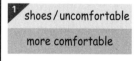
1 shoes / uncomfortable
more comfortable

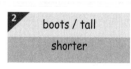
2 boots / tall
shorter

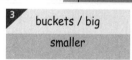
3 buckets / big
smaller

4 💡

BEST *Plus:* What do you buy when you go shopping?

52

Unit 5

All-Star 2 Study Guide

Student Name _____   Date _____

Instructor Name _____

Identify articles of clothing, U.S. sizes, quality, and prices. Student Book page 77. LCP-C 45.04 . . . . CASAS 1.1.9 . . . BEST *Plus*

WINDOW ON PRONUNCIATION 🎧
Stress

 Listen to the conversations. Then listen and repeat.

1. A: What's wrong with it?
   B: It's too tight.

2. A: Is it tight enough?
   B: It's too tight.

3. A: How is that one?
   B: It's much softer.

4. A: Is it softer?
   B: Yes, it's much softer.

Listen to the conversations again. Circle the stressed words.

 Work with a partner. Practice the conversations. Stress the important words. Circle the stressed word in each conversation.

1. A: What's wrong with it?
   B: It's too small.

2. A: Is it a heavy coat?
   B: Yes, it's too heavy.

3. A: Is this one quieter?
   B: It's much quieter.

4. A: Why do you like that one?
   B: It's much cheaper.

All-Star 2 Study Guide

Student Name _____   **Date** _____

Instructor Name _____

See Student Book page 79.

Read and discuss simple guarantees, warranties, and procedures to return merchandise. Student Book page 78.
LCP-C 45.06 . . . CASAS 1.3.3

---

2 Think About It

Answer the questions below. Use the information in Sam's Layaway Plan and the information on page 79.

1. Sara wants to buy a $120.00 vacuum at Sam's Store, but she doesn't have enough money to pay for it now. She decides to use the store layaway plan. How much money does she need to put down?

   _____

2. Tim bought a new Shark washing machine for $600.00. After six months, the machine stopped working. What should Tim do?

   _____

   _____

3. Dana is looking for a new coat and an electric coffeemaker. From the newspaper, she cut out two bonus coupons for May's Department Store. At May's, she found an $80.00 coat marked down to $50.00. She also found a coffeemaker on sale for $30.00. With the coupons, how much will she pay for the coat and the coffeemaker?

   _____

SAM'S LAYAWAY PLAN

❶ Make a 20% deposit.

❷ Full payment required in 3 months

All-Star 2 Study Guide

Student Name _____   Date _____

Instructor Name _____

C Write the amounts.

1. 50% of $100 = _____*$50.00*_____
2. 50% of $500 = _____
3. 10% of $500 = _____
4. 20% of $200 = _____
5. 10% of $35 = _____
6. 80% of $320 = _____

D Look at the chart in Activity B. Answer the questions.

1. Electric can openers are on sale at Bob's Discount House.
   They are 20% off. What price are they on sale?   _____

2. Blenders are 40% off at Best Price. What is the sale price?   _____

3. Al's Superstore is having a sale on toasters.
   They're 10% off. What's the sale price?   _____

4. Electric toothbrushes are going on sale tomorrow at Best Price.
   They are going to be 25% off. How much are they going to cost tomorrow?   _____

5. If blenders are 10% off at Best Price, are they cheaper
   than at Bob's Discount House?   _____

E Complete the chart.

WHAT 3 THINGS DO YOU NEED TO BUY SOON?	WHAT DO YOU THINK IS A GOOD PRICE FOR EACH ITEM?	WHERE ARE YOU GOING TO SHOP?

Calculate savings when items are on sale (percentage, sale price, and regular price). Workbook page 67. LCP-C 45.10 . . . CASAS 1.2.1

All-Star 2 Study Guide

Student Name _____   Date _____

Instructor Name _____

WINDOW ON GRAMMAR
Comparatives

A Read the sentences.

A broom is **cheaper** than a vacuum.
A coat is usually **more expensive** than a jacket.

ADJECTIVE	COMPARATIVE	ADJECTIVE	COMPARATIVE
cheap → cheaper		expensive → more expensive	
small → smaller		useful → more useful	
big → bigger		good → better	
nice → nicer		bad → worse	

B Complete the questions with a comparative from the list above. Then ask a classmate the questions.

1. Is a broom _____ than a mop?
2. Are boots _____ than shoes?
3. Is a toaster _____ than a blender?
4. Is a blender _____ than a can opener?

BEST *Plus:* Do you like to go shopping? Where do you like to shop?

All-Star 2 Study Guide

Student Name _____   Date _____

Instructor Name _____

Demonstrate ability to use test-taking strategies (circle, bubble in on answer sheet, true/false, and cloze). Student Book page 80.
LCP-C 49.17 . . . CASAS 7.4.7

---

1 Listening Review 🎧

Listen and choose the correct answer. Use the Answer Sheet.

1. A. It was on sale.
   B. I save ten dollars.
   C. at May's Department Store

2. A. the boots
   B. the coat
   C. the stereo

3. A. Yes, I went to the shoe store.
   B. Yes, it was on sale.
   C. Yes, I bought a new coat.

4. A. in June
   B. last year
   C. at the appliance store

5. A. Yes, they are. They're half price.
   B. Yes, they are. They are very useful.
   C. Yes, there is. It's a storewide sale.

6. A. Yes, it was heavy.
   B. Yes, it was very expensive.
   C. Yes, it was very cheap.

7. A. at Sam's Appliance Store
   B. at Gemma's Jewelry Store
   C. at Ben's Furniture Store

8. A. I like it better.
   B. It has better sales.
   C. It's better.

9. A. He's carrying a bucket.
   B. He's wearing a coat.
   C. He's going into a store.

10. A. They are 50 percent off.
    B. vacuums and coffeemakers
    C. It's the regular price.

ANSWER SHEET

	A	B	C
1	Ⓐ	Ⓑ	Ⓒ
2	Ⓐ	Ⓑ	Ⓒ
3	Ⓐ	Ⓑ	Ⓒ
4	Ⓐ	Ⓑ	Ⓒ
5	Ⓐ	Ⓑ	Ⓒ
6	Ⓐ	Ⓑ	Ⓒ
7	Ⓐ	Ⓑ	Ⓒ
8	Ⓐ	Ⓑ	Ⓒ
9	Ⓐ	Ⓑ	Ⓒ
10	Ⓐ	Ⓑ	Ⓒ

All-Star 2 Study Guide

Student Name _____   **Date** _____

Instructor Name _____

See Student Book pages 88–89.

THINGS TO DO

1 Learn New Words 🎧

Look at the menu. Listen to the words. Then listen and repeat.

- (1) appetizers
- (2) soups
- (3) salads
- (4) main dishes
- (5) sandwiches
- (6) side orders
- (7) desserts
- (8) beverages

Write the words on the lines in the menu.

2 Practice the Conversation 🎧

Listen to the conversation. Then listen and repeat.

A: Are you ready to order?

B: Yes. I'd like a small onion soup and a chicken sandwich .

A: Do you want something to drink with your sandwich ?

B: Yes. I'd like some tea , please.

A: Large or small?

B: Small , please.

Practice the conversation. Ask about these things.

1	the fish stew and a side order of fries
	your stew
	a cup of tea / Large

2	the hamburger special and a small garden salad
	your hamburger
	an orange soda / Small

3	the stuffed mushrooms and a large vegetable soup
	your soup
	a root beer / Large

4	

3 Interview

Interview a partner. Write your partner's answers.

WHAT'S YOUR FAVORITE _____ ?

kind of soup   _____

kind of sandwich   _____

vegetable   _____

dessert   _____

BEST Plus: What do you think about the American diet? Is American food healthy? Some people think American fruit and vegetables look good but don't taste good: do you agree?

All-Star 2 Study Guide

Student Name _____   Date _____

Instructor Name _____

A List holidays in the United States and in another country you know.

U.S. HOLIDAYS	HOLIDAYS IN ANOTHER COUNTRY
Fourth of July / Independence Day	*Independence Day*

B Write a paragraph about your favorite U.S. holiday.

_____

_____

_____

_____

_____

_____

_____

_____

_____

_____

BEST *Plus:* Describe your favorite holiday in your country.

Unit 6   **59**

Recognize vocabulary and traditions associated with major U.S. holidays and contrast with native customs. *BEST Plus: Describe holidays and customs in one's native country.* LCP-C 46.04 . . . CASAS 2.7.1 . . . BEST *Plus*

All-Star 2 Study Guide

Student Name _____   **Date** _____

Instructor Name _____

WINDOW ON PRONUNCIATION 🎧
Intonation Patterns in Sentences and Questions

 Listen to the sentences. Then listen and repeat.

1. I'd like a large salad and a coffee.
2. I'd like a veggie sandwich, a salad and a root beer.
3. I'd like the onion soup, an order of fries, and a chicken sandwich.
4. For here or to go?
5. Large or small?

 Listen to the conversations. Then listen and repeat.

1. Waiter: Do you want french fries or a salad?
   Customer: French fries.

2. Waiter: Do you want french fries or a salad?
   Customer: Sure. I'll take a salad.

3. Waiter: Would you like cake or ice cream?
   Customer: Cake, please.

4. Waiter: Would you like cake or ice cream?
   Customer: No, thanks. I'm too full.

⭐ Work with a partner. Take turns asking and answering the questions from Activity B.

All-Star 2 Study Guide

Student Name _____   Date _____

Instructor Name _____

See Student Book pages 90–91.

THINGS TO DO

1 Learn New Words 🎧

Look at the pictures. Listen to the words. Then listen and repeat.

- ① fry
- ② bake
- ③ boil
- ④ cut up
- ⑤ slice
- ⑥ mix
- ⑦ form a ball
- ⑧ roll
- ⑨ heat

Which words are new to you? Circle them.

2 Read and Number the Pictures

Read the recipe on page 91. Number the pictures below from first (1) to last (5).

Use the pictures. Retell the instructions without looking at the recipe on page 91.

3 Write

Write the ingredients and instructions for a dish you like. Then share your recipe with the class.

★ ★

TRY THIS Use a search engine to find a recipe for something you want to make. Bring the recipe you find to class to share.

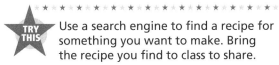

chocolate cake   Search

★ ★

Write a set of simple directions. Student Book page 90. LCP-C 49.14

All-Star 2 Study Guide

Student Name _____   **Date** _____

Instructor Name _____

See Student Book pages 84–85.

Use nouns (count, non-count). Student Book page 84. LCP-C 50.07 ... BEST *Plus*

THINGS TO DO

1 Learn New Words 🎧

Look at the pictures. Listen to the words. Then listen and repeat.

1. red meat
2. poultry
3. fish
4. eggs
5. milk
6. ice cream
7. cheese
8. oil
9. fruit
10. peanuts
11. vegetables
12. sugar
13. flour
14. cereal
15. soft drinks
16. coffee

Which words are new to you? Circle them.

2 Check *True* or *False*

Study the bar graph and read the sentences below. Check (✓) *True* or *False*. Then correct the false sentences.

	True	False
1. Americans eat about 325 pounds of fruit a year.	☐	☐
2. Americans eat 50 pounds of vegetables a year.	☐	☐
3. Americans eat more red meat than poultry.	☐	☐
4. Americans eat more fruit than vegetables.	☐	☐
5. Americans drink about 10 pounds of coffee a year.	☐	☐

3 Interview

Work with a partner. Ask your partner the questions below. Record your partner's answers.

A: Did you eat any fish yesterday?

B: Yes, I did. I had fish for dinner.

A: Did you eat any eggs yesterday?

B: No, I didn't.

Did you eat any _____ yesterday?	Yes, I did. I had _____ for _____.				No, I didn't.
	breakfast	lunch	dinner	a snack	
fish	☐	☐	☐	☐	☐
red meat	☐	☐	☐	☐	☐
fruit	☐	☐	☐	☐	☐
vegetables	☐	☐	☐	☐	☐
_____	☐	☐	☐	☐	☐

All-Star 2 Study Guide for Post-Testing Copyright © McGraw-Hill

All-Star 2 Study Guide

Student Name _____   Date _____

Instructor Name _____

See Student Book pages 84–85.

WINDOW ON GRAMMAR
Using *How much* and *How many*

A Read the questions. Check (✓) your answers.

Count Nouns (Things you can count)	a lot	a few	none
How many eggs did you eat last week?	☐	☐	☐
How many apples did you eat?	☐	☐	☐

Noncount Nouns (Things you can't count)	a lot	a little	none
How much meat did you eat last week?	☐	☐	☐
How much coffee do you drink?	☐	☐	☐

B Complete the questions. Write *How much* or *How many*. Then ask a classmate the questions.

1. _____ peanuts can you eat?
2. _____ sugar do you put on your cereal?
3. _____ ice cream did you eat last week?
4. _____ fruit did you eat yesterday?
5. _____ eggs do you eat in a week?

Use nouns (count, non-count). Student Book page 85. LCP-C 50.07 . . . BEST *Plus*

All-Star 2 Study Guide

Student Name _____ **Date** _____

Instructor Name _____

See Student Book pages 98–99.

1 Read the restaurant review questionnaire. Answer the question below.

RESTAURANT REVIEW QUESTIONNAIRE

What's the name of the restaurant? _Tippy's Lunch_

What kind of food does it serve? _American_

How many people does it seat? _35_

	Yes	No
Is it clean?	☑	☐
Is it expensive?	☐	☑
Are children welcome?	☑	☐
Does it have good service?	☑	☐
Are the waiters friendly?	☑	☐
Does it have take out?	☑	☐
Is the food good?	☑	☐

Other: _not many healthy options_

FOCUS ON WRITING: Writing A Review

A good restaurant review uses descriptive language to help readers learn about the service, food, and price. Descriptive language includes adjectives that give interesting information. These adjectives help readers know if you like or dislike a restaurant.

EXAMPLES: **great** meatloaf
low prices
friendly waiters
unhealthy items

Do you want to go to Tippy's Lunch? Why or why not?

_____

_____

2 Read the restaurant review. Answer the questions.

Restaurant Reviews

Tippy's Lunch

Tippy's Lunch is a great place for a meal. It has great meatloaf, green beans, and mashed potatoes, all for low prices. It also has wonderful appetizers, burgers, chili, and soups. I really liked the friendly waiters and the fast service. Also, children are welcome. Tippy's is not the place to eat if you are on a diet. There are many unhealthy items on the menu. But if you want to eat great-tasting food, Tippy's is the place.

Service ★ ★ ★ ★
Food ★ ★ ★
Price $

1. Is Tippy's Lunch expensive?

_____

2. What food is good at Tippy's?

_____

_____

3. What is one problem with the food choices at Tippy's?

_____

_____

All-Star 2 Study Guide

Student Name _____ Date _____

Instructor Name _____

See Student Book pages 98–99.

3 Complete the questionnaire about a restaurant you know.

RESTAURANT REVIEW QUESTIONNAIRE

What's the name of the restaurant? _____

What kind of food does it serve? _____

How many people does it seat? _____

	Yes	No
Is it clean?	❏	❏
Is it expensive?	❏	❏
Are children welcome?	❏	❏
Does it have good service?	❏	❏
Are the waiters friendly?	❏	❏
Does it have take out?	❏	❏
Is the food good?	❏	❏

Other: _____

_____

4 Write a review about the restaurant. Use descriptive language to tell if you like or dislike the restaurant.

_____ (name of the restaurant)

_____

_____

_____

_____

_____

_____

Service

Food

Price

Recognize, state, read, and write statements and questions. Student Book page 99. LCP-C 49.01

All-Star 2 Study Guide

Student Name _____   Date _____

Instructor Name _____

A Read the information about planning an event for work. Complete the sentences below.

> **What you need to find out first**
>
> Before you talk to your caterer about the food, answer these questions.
>
> **1.** How many people will attend the event?
>
> **2.** What kind of event is it? Will you serve dinner?
>
> **3.** If you are serving appetizers, do you want light, medium, or heavy appetizers (light=snack, medium=possible meal, heavy=a meal)?
>
> **4.** What types of beverages? Hot or cold?
>
> **5.** Is it a sit-down meal? Do you want square or round tables?
>
> **7.** Are there any colors you prefer?
>
> **8.** Do you need flowers or balloons?

1. A _____ caterer _____ is someone who takes care of the food for an event.

2. You need to know how many _____ will attend.

3. You should decide if you want hot or cold _____.

4. There are three types of _____: light, medium, and heavy.

5. You can get square or round _____.

6. You need to decide if you want _____ or

   _____ for the room.

B Answer the questions about you.

1. What was the last special work event you went to?

   _____

2. What kind of food did they have?

   _____

All-Star 2 Study Guide

Student Name _____   Date _____

Instructor Name _____

C Read the form. Match the questions and answers below.

Big City Caterers

Welcome to Big City Caterers Online Registration

First name:	Linda	Last name:	Muhammad
Date of event:	3/12/2007	Location:	Bainbridge Hall
Set up time:	3:30 p.m.	Time of event:	6:00 p.m.
Email address:	lmuhammad@hamiltonpress.com	Telephone:	(617)555-9002

Comments/questions:

Company awards banquet. Sit-down dinner with round tables. Servers to pass light appetizers.
Cold beverages with the meal, hot beverages after the meal.

Questions

1. What is Linda's last name?
2. Where is the event?
3. What is the event?
4. What time does the event begin?
5. What is Linda's phone number?

Answers

a. (617) 555-9002
b. Muhammad
c. 6 o'clock
d. company awards banquet
e. Bainbridge Hall

★ ★

TAKE IT OUTSIDE: Interview a family member, friend, or coworker. Ask about a future or past event.
Complete the form.

Big City Caterers

Welcome to Big City Caterers Online Registration

First name:		Last name:	
Date of event:		Location:	
Set up time:		Time of event:	
Email address:		Telephone:	

Comments/questions:

★ ★

Demonstrate ability to describe a person, place, thing, or event. Workbook page 89. LCP-C 49.03 ... BEST *Plus*

All-Star 2 Study Guide

Student Name _____   Date _____

Instructor Name _____

Demonstrate appropriate communication skills in the work environment (interactions with supervisor and co-workers). Workbook page 103. LCP-C 36.05 . . . CASAS 4.8.1, 4.8.2

A Read the statements about communicating at work. Check *True, False,* or *I don't know.*

1. You shouldn't ask too many questions.   ☐ True   ☐ False   ☐ I don't know.
2. You should get upset at criticism.   ☐ True   ☐ False   ☐ I don't know.
3. You shouldn't give ideas to others.   ☐ True   ☐ False   ☐ I don't know.
4. You should compliment others.   ☐ True   ☐ False   ☐ I don't know.
5. You should be positive.   ☐ True   ☐ False   ☐ I don't know.

B Complete the sentences.

1. If someone upsets you at work, _____ .

2. If you aren't sure what to do, _____ .

3. If someone criticizes you, _____ .

4. If a coworker does a good job, _____ .

5. If a coworker is sick, _____ .

C List 3 ideas you will try to get along with people better at work or school.

1. _____

2. _____

3. _____

★ ★

TAKE IT OUTSIDE: Interview a family member, friend, or coworker. Complete the survey.

AT WORK OR SCHOOL, HOW OFTEN DO YOU _____ ?	NEVER	SOMETIMES	ALWAYS
ask questions when you don't understand something			
get upset when someone says something negative			
compliment others on their good work			
ask for more information when you are criticized			
offer to help others			

★ ★

All-Star 2 Study Guide for Post-Testing Copyright © McGraw-Hill

All-Star 2 Study Guide

Student Name _____   **Date** _____

Instructor Name _____

See Student Book pages 100–101.

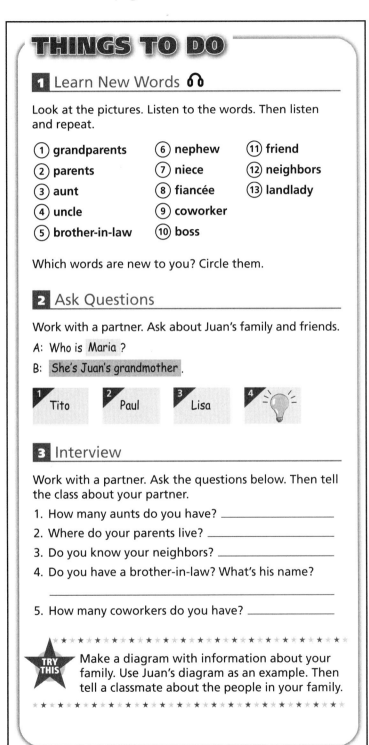

THINGS TO DO

1 Learn New Words 🎧

Look at the pictures. Listen to the words. Then listen and repeat.

① grandparents   ⑥ nephew   ⑪ friend
② parents   ⑦ niece   ⑫ neighbors
③ aunt   ⑧ fiancée   ⑬ landlady
④ uncle   ⑨ coworker
⑤ brother-in-law   ⑩ boss

Which words are new to you? Circle them.

2 Ask Questions

Work with a partner. Ask about Juan's family and friends.

A: Who is Maria ?
B: She's Juan's grandmother .

1 Tito   2 Paul   3 Lisa   4 💡

3 Interview

Work with a partner. Ask the questions below. Then tell the class about your partner.

1. How many aunts do you have? _____
2. Where do your parents live? _____
3. Do you know your neighbors? _____
4. Do you have a brother-in-law? What's his name?

   _____

5. How many coworkers do you have? _____

★ ★

TRY THIS Make a diagram with information about your family. Use Juan's diagram as an example. Then tell a classmate about the people in your family.

★ ★

Describe self, family members, and others (physical characteristics and personal traits). *BEST Plus: Describe family members and describe family traditions.* Student Book page 100. LCP-C 39.02 … CASAS 0.1.4, 0.2.1 … BEST Plus

BEST *Plus*: Describe someone in your family. What do you usually do to celebrate a holiday?

All-Star 2 Study Guide

Student Name _____   **Date** _____

Instructor Name _____

See Student Book pages 104–105.

Use appropriate expressions to express feelings and emotions. BEST Plus: Describe preferences about fun and entertainment. Student Book page 104. LCP-C 39.03 . . . BEST Plus

THINGS TO DO

1 Learn New Words 🎧

Look at the pictures. Listen to the words. Then listen and repeat.

(1) ask for advice   (4) apologize   (7) criticize

(2) take care of   (5) disagree   (8) talk back

(3) compliment   (6) yell at

2 Ask Questions

Work with a partner. Take turns asking these questions.

DID YOU _____ YESTERDAY?	YES	NO	WHO?
ask anyone* for advice	☐	☐	_____
take care of anyone	☐	☐	_____
compliment anyone	☐	☐	_____
apologize to anyone	☐	☐	_____
disagree with anyone	☐	☐	_____
criticize anyone	☐	☐	_____

*Note: *anyone* means *any person.*

3 Practice the Conversation 🎧

Listen to the conversation. Then listen and repeat.

A: How was your day?

B: Not so good.

A: What happened?

B: My boss criticized me.

A: That's too bad. What did he say?

B: He said I was very disorganized .

Practice the conversation with a partner. Use these ideas.

1 Great. / My boss complimented my writing.	**2** Terrible. / A man yelled at me.	**3** Awful. / My son talked back to me.
That's wonderful.	Really?	Really?
it was very nice	I should slow down	he didn't want to study

BEST *Plus:* Look at Student Book page 103. What are the people doing? What do you like to do? What do you usually do for fun?

All-Star 2 Study Guide for Post-Testing Copyright © McGraw-Hill

All-Star 2 Study Guide

Student Name _____ **Date** _____

Instructor Name _____

All-Star 2 Study Guide for Post-Testing Copyright © McGraw-Hill

1 Learn New Words 🎧

Listen to the words for items you can mail. Then listen and repeat.

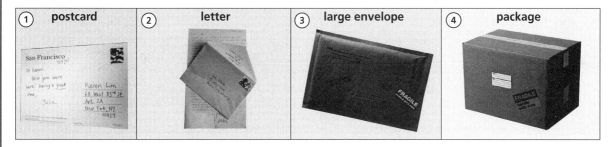

| ① postcard | ② letter | ③ large envelope | ④ package |

2 Read and Check *True* or *False*

Look at the chart. Read the questions below about U.S. postal services. Check (✓) *True* or *False*.

Service	Items You Can Mail	Cost	Speed
Express Mail	letter large envelope package (70 lbs. or less)	$$$ based on weight	1–2 days guaranteed
Priority Mail	large envelope package (70 lbs. or less)	$$ based on weight and distance if over 1 pound	1–3 days
First-Class Mail	postcard letter large envelope package (13 oz. or less)	$ based on weight	1–3 days
Parcel Post	package (70 lbs. or less)	$ based on weight and distance	2–9 days

1. Parcel post is the slowest way to send a package.   ☐ True   ☐ False
2. First-class mail is the most expensive way to send a letter.   ☐ True   ☐ False
3. Express mail is the fastest way to send a letter.   ☐ True   ☐ False
4. You can send a letter by parcel post.   ☐ True   ☐ False

Identify procedures for mailing a letter or package (domestic/international), purchasing money orders, and registering mail. Student Book page 110. LCP-C 46.02 . . . CASAS 2.4.2, 2.4.6

All-Star 2 Study Guide

Student Name _____   **Date** _____

Instructor Name _____

See Student Book pages 110–111.

Identify procedures for mailing a letter or package (domestic/international), purchasing money orders, and registering mail. Student Book page 111. LCP-C 46.02 . . . CASAS 2.4.2, 2.4.6

3 Evaluate

Choose the best postal service for each situation below.

Situation #1	Situation #2	Situation #3
David is in New York. He has to send a package to his boss in California. She is making a presentation there in two days. It is important that the package is on time. The cost is not important.	Marta is mailing her brother's wedding invitations. Her brother is getting married in two months. The invitations are in small envelopes. She wants the invitations to arrive in a few days.	Julie is sending two packages. One is a wedding present for a friend. The other is a graduation present for her cousin. She has lots of time. Both packages are over 2 pounds.
Best Way to Mail It	Best Way to Mail Them	Best Way to Mail Them
Reason	Reason	Reason

WINDOW ON MATH
Ounces and Pounds

16 ounces (oz.) = 1 pound (lb.)

 A Answer these questions.

1. Your package weighs 5 pounds. How many ounces does it weigh?

2. You have to send a package that weighs 18 oz. Which U.S. postal services can you use?

3. Your package weighs 48 oz. If it costs $1.50 per lb. to mail it, how much does it cost?

4. The maximum weight for a package is 70 lbs. How many ounces is that?

All-Star 2 Study Guide for Post-Testing Copyright © McGraw-Hill

All-Star 2 Study Guide

Student Name _____ Date _____

Instructor Name _____

A Read the letters. Complete the chart below.

Dear Dr. Dina,

I have two children, a son and a daughter. My son is 6 years old and my daughter is 4. Sometimes I have trouble handling their behavior. My son sometimes hits his sister when they are playng together. My daughter doesn't listen to me. For example, if I tell her to stop playing with her food, she still plays. I get so angry with them. What should I do?

Sincerely, Mad Mom

Dear Mad Mom,

It's hard to know how to discipline our children sometimes. You are a parent and your job is to keep children safe and help them learn. Children need to know how to follow rules. Here are some guidelines:

• Use simple rules.
• Help your children use words. Teach your son how to tell his sister what he wants instead of hitting her.
• If you ignore small problems, they may go away. For example, compliment your daughter when she is eating properly, and ignore her when she plays with her food.
• Use time outs. Sometimes just taking your child away from the situation works.
• Reward good behavior.
I hope these ideas help.

Dr. Dina

PROBLEMS (MAD MOM'S)	SOLUTIONS (DR. DINA'S IDEAS)

B Answer the questions.

1. How many children does the mother have? _____

2. What are the ages of the children? _____

3. What is the son's problem? _____

4. What is the daughter's problem? _____

5. Why is the mother writing? _____

6. What does Dr. Dina say a parent's job is? _____

Recognize the importance of proper child care and acceptable discipline (requirement of food, shelter, hygiene, child care providers). Workbook page 100. LCP-C 48.04. …CASAS 2.5.9, 3.5.7

All-Star 2 Study Guide

Student Name _____   **Date** _____

Instructor Name _____

Recognize the importance of proper child care and acceptable discipline (requirement of food, shelter, hygiene, child care providers). Workbook page 101. LCP-C 48.04 . . . CASAS 2.5.9, 3.5.7

C Look at the picture. Answer the question below.

Is this a discipline problem? What would you do?

_____

_____

★ ★

TAKE IT OUTSIDE: Interview a family member, friend, or coworker. Write the answers.

1. What behavior problems do your children have? _____

   _____

2. How do you discipline your children? _____

   _____

★ ★

TAKE IT ONLINE: Search on the Internet using the words "disciplining children." Write down 2 ideas and share them with your classmates.

All-Star 2 Study Guide

Student Name _____   Date _____

Instructor Name _____

C Look at the family tree diagram. Answer the questions below.

whose/who's

female ◯   male ☐

```
                    Donna ──── Richard
                         │
            ┌────────────┴────────────┐
      Maria ─── Ivan            Isha ─── Jerome
            │
      ┌─────┴─────┐
    Anita       Scott
```

1. Who's Ivan's sister?   _____

2. Whose wife is Maria?   _____

3. Who's Scott's grandfather?   _____

4. Whose niece is Anita?   _____

5. Whose husband is Jerome?   _____

D Answer the questions about you.

1. Where do your parents live?   _____

2. How many uncles do you have?   _____

3. Whose son or daughter are you?   _____

4. Are your neighbors friendly?   _____

5. Who's your best friend?   _____

6. Who was your favorite boss?   _____

7. Who's your father?   _____

8. Whose parent are you?   _____

9. Whose neighbor are you?   _____

Demonstrate ability to read and understand basic charts, graphs, maps, tables, and diagrams. Workbook page 93.
LCP-C 49.09 . . . CASAS 2.5.4, 6.6.5

All-Star 2 Study Guide

Student Name _____   Date _____

Instructor Name _____

See Student Book pages 102–103.

Demonstrate ability to use test-taking strategies (circle, bubble in on answer sheet, true/false, and cloze). Teacher's Edition page 239.
LCP-C 49.17 . . . CASAS 7.4.7

Reading: Sylvia's Story

A. Read Sylvia's story. Check *True* or *False*.

My name is Sylvia. Today my daughter Lisa is getting married. It is a very happy day for my family. I remember my own wedding day. I wore a long white dress. When I married Ron, we had a formal dinner. The guests sat at round tables and waiters served the food. We also had music. One musician played the piano and another played the violin. I danced with my father for the first dance. Later, the musicians played a special song for my husband and me, and we danced too. About 200 guests came to our wedding, and they all brought gifts. Our wedding was at night. Because it was a formal wedding, we did not invite children. We had a beautiful pink and white wedding cake.

1. Sylvia is getting married today.	☐ True	☐ False
2. Sylvia wore a white dress at her wedding.	☐ True	☐ False
3. Sylvia has a daughter.	☐ True	☐ False
4. Sylvia danced with her father at her wedding.	☐ True	☐ False
5. Sylvia's husband's name is Juan.	☐ True	☐ False
6. Her daughter's name is Lisa.	☐ True	☐ False

B. Look at the big picture. Complete the chart. Write three more things in each column.

At Sylvia's Wedding	At Both Sylvia's and Lisa's Weddings	At Lisa's Wedding
Waiters served the food.	The bride wore a white dress.	The food was on a big table.

All-Star 2 Study Guide

Student Name _____   Date _____

Instructor Name _____

Use nouns (count, non-count). Student Book page 115. LCP-C 50.07 . . . BEST *Plus*

COUNT NOUNS AND NONCOUNT NOUNS

Count Nouns	*Noncount Nouns*
• Count nouns have a singular and a plural form. EXAMPLES: student—students brother—brothers	• Noncount nouns are always singular. EXAMPLES: money furniture music coffee
• You can use *a* or *an* with the singular form of count nouns. EXAMPLES: a brother, an aunt, a family	• You don't use *a* or *an* with noncount nouns. EXAMPLES: I like music. I love coffee.
• You can use *many, a lot of, a few,* and *any* with the plural form of count nouns. EXAMPLE: I have many aunts, a lot of cousins, and a few nieces. I don't have any nephews.	• You can use *much, a lot of, a little,* and *any* with noncount nouns. EXAMPLE: I drank too much coffee. I ate a lot of fruit and a little meat. I didn't eat any bread.
	• We often use quantity words with noncount nouns. EXAMPLE: I drank a cup of coffee. I bought a loaf of bread.

3 Read the sentences. Is the **boldfaced** word a count noun or a noncount noun? Write *C* (count noun) or *NC* (noncount noun) next to each question.

1. Do you have any **sisters**? _C_
2. Do you have any **furniture**? _____
3. Do you have a lot of **work**? _____
4. Do you have a lot of **friends**? _____
5. Do you have a few **stamps**? _____
6. Do you have a little **milk**? _____
7. Do you have some **sugar**? _____
8. Do you have some **envelopes**? _____
9. Do you have a **telephone** at home? _____
10. Do you have **electricity** at home? _____
11. Do you have **chairs** at home? _____
12. How much **money** did it cost? _____
13. How many **packages** did you send? _____
14. Do you want a **bowl** of cereal? _____

4 Complete the sentences. Choose the correct word in parentheses.

1. Did you buy many _____? (books / furniture)
2. He bought _____ stamps at the post office. (a few / a little)
3. She is putting _____ milk in her coffee. (a few / a little)
4. A lot of chairs _____ empty. (is / are)
5. Some clothing _____ on sale this week. (is / are)
6. How _____ tea do you want? (many / much)
7. How _____ students are in your class? (many / much)
8. Do you want _____ cup of coffee? (a / some)

All-Star 2 Study Guide

Student Name _____   Date _____

Instructor Name _____

See Student Book pages 116–117.

Identify body parts and the five senses. Student Book page 116. LCP-C 41.01 . . . CASAS 3.1.1

THINGS TO DO

1 Learn New Words 🎧

Look at the pictures. Listen to the words. Then listen and repeat.

- ① brain
- ② tooth*
- ③ muscle
- ④ waist
- ⑤ hip
- ⑥ joint
- ⑦ bone
- ⑧ skin
- ⑨ blood
- ⑩ heart
- ⑪ lungs
- ⑫ back

*Note: the plural of *tooth* is *teeth*.

Write the new words on the lines.

2 Write

Complete the chart with parts of the body for each category below. Then compare lists with a partner.

I have muscles in my _____.	I have bones in my _____.	My _____ is a joint.
1. _____arm_____	1. _____finger_____	1. _____shoulder_____
2. _____	2. _____	2. _____
3. _____	3. _____	3. _____
4. _____	4. _____	
5. _____	5. _____	

3 Check Your Answers

Read the statements. Check (✓) *True, False,* or *I don't know.* Then correct the false statements.

	True	False	I don't know
1. You breathe with your lungs.	☐	☐	☐
2. Your elbow is between your shoulder and wrist.	☐	☐	☐
3. An ankle is a joint.	☐	☐	☐
4. You have skin on your teeth.	☐	☐	☐
5. Your heart moves your blood around.	☐	☐	☐
6. You have more bones than teeth.	☐	☐	☐
7. Two bones meet at a joint.	☐	☐	☐
8. Your brain is a muscle.	☐	☐	☐

All-Star 2 Study Guide for Post-Testing Copyright © McGraw-Hill

All-Star 2 Study Guide

Student Name _____   Date _____

Instructor Name _____

See Student Book pages 118–119.

Describe aches, pains, illnesses, injuries, dental health problems, and follow doctor's instructions. *BEST Plus: Describe methods of treating common illnesses or maladies.* Student Book page 118. LCP-C 41.03 . . . CASAS 3.1.1 . . . BEST *Plus*

THINGS TO DO

1 Learn New Words 🎧

Look at the pictures. Listen to the words. Then listen and repeat.

1. burn
2. cut
3. fracture
4. sprain
5. bruise
6. shock
7. rash
8. fever
9. cold
10. flu
11. infection
12. feel dizzy
13. blister
14. feel nauseous
15. bleed

Which words are new to you? Circle them.

2 Practice the Conversation 🎧

Listen to the conversation. Then listen and repeat.

A: Is your rash getting any better?
B: No, I don't think so.
A: Maybe you should see a doctor.
B: Maybe you're right.

Practice the conversation with a partner. Ask about these things.

1 cold/get some medicine	2 fever/drink more liquids	3 sprain/put ice on it
4 head cold/lie down	5 cut/go to the doctor	6 💡

3 Write

Complete the sentences below. Then compare ideas with the class.

1. You should go to the doctor if ____*you have a high fever*____.
2. You should rest if _____.
3. You should stay off your feet if _____.
4. You should stay at home if _____.
5. You should _____ if you have a cold.

★ ★

TRY THIS Use the Internet or your local phone book to find information about health services in your area. Write down the address and phone number of a clinic and a hospital near you.

★ ★

BEST *Plus:* Some people think herbal tea is good for a cold. What do you think? What are some things that people can do to stay healthy? What foods do you think are good to eat when you're sick? Why?

All-Star 2 Study Guide

Student Name _____   Date _____

Instructor Name _____

Describe aches, pains, illnesses, injuries, dental health problems, and follow doctor's instructions. *BEST Plus: Describe methods of treating common illnesses or maladies.* Workbook page 110. LCP-C 41.03 . . . CASAS 3.1.1 . . . BEST Plus

A Match the questions and answers.

Questions	Answers
1. _____ My skin is red. What's wrong with it?	a. I fell down the stairs.
2. _____ How do I know when I have the flu?	b. You might get a burn.
3. _____ What's a fracture?	c. Your joints ache, you have a fever, and you feel terrible.
4. _____ How did you get that bruise?	d. It looks like a rash.
5. _____ What will happen if you touch the hot stove?	e. It's a broken bone.

B Circle the correct answer.

1. I cut my finger and now it's red and smells bad. I think I have:

   A. an infection.   B. a sprain.

2. Jorge fell and turned his ankle. He might have:

   A. the flu.   B. a sprain.

3. My sister ate something bad. Now she is:

   A. bleeding.   B. feeling nauseous.

4. My new shoes are too tight. They're giving me:

   A. a cold.   B. a blister.

5. Don't touch that electric wire. You might get:

   A. a shock.   B. a bruise.

C Answer the questions about you.

1. Did you have the flu last year?   _____

2. Do you have a fever today?   _____

3. Are you feeling dizzy now?   _____

4. When do you feel nauseous?   _____

5. How often do you get a cold?   _____

All-Star 2 Study Guide for Post-Testing Copyright © McGraw-Hill

All-Star 2 Study Guide

Student Name _____   Date _____

Instructor Name _____

See Student Book pages 122–123.

THINGS TO DO

1 Learn New Words 🎧

Look at the medicine labels. Listen to the words. Then listen and repeat.

① tablet   ② teaspoon   ③ cream   ④ OTC   ⑤ capsule

2 Read and Take Notes

Read the labels and complete the chart below.

Name of medicine	Form	How much?	How often?
A. *acetaminophen*	*tablet*		every 46 hours
B.	*liquid*		
C. *hydrocortisone*		-----	
D.		*1*	

3 Check *True* or *False*

Read the statements. Check (✓) *True* or *False*. Then correct the false statements.

		True	False
1.	Children older than six can take acetaminophen.	☐	☐
2.	You can swallow hydrocortisone cream.	☐	☐
3.	Children under age 12 can take Max-Relief.	☐	☐
4.	Ampicillin and Max-Relief are OTC.	☐	☐
5.	Dr. Dickinson prescribed the hydrocortisone.	☐	☐
6.	The ampicillin is for Claire Donnalley.	☐	☐
7.	You can use the ampicillin in 2008.	☐	☐
8.	Acetaminophen is a prescription medicine.	☐	☐

4 Write

Make a chart like this. Write the health problem or symptom next to the medicine.

NAME OF MEDICINE	USE THE MEDICINE FOR THESE PROBLEMS
Acetaminophen	headache, backache, …
Max-Relief	
Hydrocortisone	

BEST *Plus:* Where do you get your medicine? What do you take when you have a headache?

Unit 8   **81**

Read and interpret medical instructions for prescriptions and over the counter drugs. *BEST Plus: Read and interpret information on medicine labels.* Student Book page 122. LCP-C 41.04 … CASAS 3.1.1, 3.3.2, 3.3.3 … BEST *Plus*

All-Star 2 Study Guide

Student Name _____   Date _____

Instructor Name _____

A Read the medical history form. Answer the questions below.

Medical History Form

Name: Last	First	MI	Birthdate	Sex
Park	Grace	S.	5/19/72	Female

Address	City	State	Zip
6517 South Elm St.	Bradford	MI	49503

Person to notify in case of emergency	Relationship	Telephone number
Elizabeth Park	sister	555-8043

	Age	Occupation	Significant medical problems
Father	62	store owner	heart disease
Mother	59	accountant	none
Sister	27	dentist	bad headaches
Brother	37	librarian	none

Have you had any of the following? Check *yes* or *no*. Explain if you answer *yes*.

Heart problems _____ ☐ yes ☐ no

Lung problems _____ ☐ yes ☐ no

Bleeding problems _____ ☐ yes ☐ no

Bad headaches _____ ☐ yes ☐ no

Repeated infections _____ ☐ yes ☐ no

Repeated earaches I get earaches several times a year. ☑ yes ☐ no

Allergies _____ ☐ yes ☐ no

1. What is the patient's name? _____

2. What is her father's health problem? _____

3. Does her mother have a health problem? _____

4. Who should someone call if there is an emergency? _____

5. What problem does the patient sometimes have? _____

All-Star 2 Study Guide

Student Name _____   Date _____

Instructor Name _____

B Complete the medical history form for you.

Medical History Form

Name: Last		First	MI	Birthdate	Sex

Address		City		State	Zip

Person to notify in case of emergency			Relationship	Telephone number

	Age	Occupation	Significant medical problems
Father			
Mother			
Sister			
Brother			

Have you had any of the following? Check *yes* or *no*. Explain if you answer *yes*.

Heart problems _____ ☐ yes ☐ no

Lung problems _____ ☐ yes ☐ no

Bleeding problems _____ ☐ yes ☐ no

Bad headaches _____ ☐ yes ☐ no

Repeated infections _____ ☐ yes ☐ no

Repeated earaches _____ ☐ yes ☐ no

Allergies _____ ☐ yes ☐ no

Fill out medical history form. Workbook page 117. LCP-C 41.07 . . . CASAS 3.2.1

★ ★

TAKE IT OUTSIDE: Interview a family member, friend, or coworker. Write the answers.

1. What kind of health problems do you have?

_____

2. Did you have any serious injuries when you were a child? If yes, what were they?

_____

3. Does anyone in your family have serious health problems?

_____

★ ★

All-Star 2 Study Guide

Student Name _____   **Date** _____

Instructor Name _____

Compare services provided by the health department, hospitals, emergency rooms, and clinics. Workbook page 118.
LCP-C 41.05 . . . CASAS 3.1.3

A Read about health care services. Circle the words that are new to you.

| convulsion | numbness | urgent | vomiting |

When should you go to an emergency room?

Go to the emergency room when you have a serious medical condition or symptom (including severe pain) caused by an injury or illness, which happens suddenly. The ER is for situations where you may die if you don't get treatment right away.

Some examples include:

- Signs of a heart attack that last two minutes or longer, including chest pain
- Signs of stroke, like sudden onset of numbness in arms or legs
- Severe shortness of breath
- Bleeding that won't stop
- Poisoning
- Bad fractures
- Major injury such as head injury
- Coughing up or vomiting blood

When can you go to an urgent care center?

"Urgent care" is care that can wait for the time it takes to call your doctor for instructions on treatment. Your doctor can tell you if you should go to an urgent care center or come to the office.

Examples of problems your doctor or an urgent care center can treat:

- Earaches
- Minor cuts where bleeding is controlled
- Sprains
- Skin rashes
- Colds, coughs, sore throat
- Most fevers, though if there is a convulsion or extreme fever in a child, go to the ER

If you have any questions about whether it is an emergency or not, you should call your primary care physician.

B Write the definitions.

The emergency room: _____

An urgent care center: _____

All-Star 2 Study Guide for Post-Testing Copyright © McGraw-Hill

All-Star 2 Study Guide

Student Name _____   Date _____

Instructor Name _____

See Workbook page 118.

C Check *the emergency room* or *an urgent care center*.

IF YOU HAVE THIS PROBLEM, YOU SHOULD GO TO:	THE EMERGENCY ROOM	AN URGENT CARE CENTER
a heart attack		
an earache		
severe bleeding that won't stop		
a bad cold		
a bad fracture		

D Answer the questions.

1. If you have the flu, should you go to the emergency room or call your doctor?

   _____

2. If you cut your hand and you can't stop the bleeding, where should you go?

   _____

3. What might happen if you have a heart attack and you don't go to the emergency room?

   _____

4. Which do you think you should use more often, the emergency room or an urgent care center?

   _____

★ ★

TAKE IT OUTSIDE: Interview a family member, friend, or coworker. Write the answers.

1. Do you ever go to the emergency room at the hospital? Why or why not?

   _____

   _____

★ ★

TAKE IT ONLINE: Search the Internet for the names of 2 hospitals with emergency rooms and 2 urgent care centers in your area. Write the names and addresses. Keep the information where you can find it quickly in an emergency.

Compare services provided by the health department, hospitals, emergency rooms, and clinics. Workbook page 119.
LCP-C 41.05 . . . CASAS 3.1.3

All-Star 2 Study Guide

Student Name _____   **Date** _____

Instructor Name _____

See Student Book pages 120–121.

Demonstrate procedures for first aid (assess individual's condition, procedures to follow after assessment, including calling 911 or administering first aid for minor situations). Student Book page 120. LCP-C 41.09 . . . CASAS 3.1.1, 3.4.3, 3.4.5

THINGS TO DO

1 Learn New Words

Look at the picture. Listen to the words. Then listen and repeat.

1. emergency room
2. examining room
3. x-ray
4. radiology
5. stitches
6. sling
7. ice pack
8. admissions desk
9. splint
10. wheelchair
11. waiting room
12. crutches
13. cast
14. bandage

Which words are new to you? Circle them.

2 Talk About the Picture

Write 5 questions about the picture. Then ask your classmates your questions.

> EXAMPLES: What is wrong with Lupe's child?
> Who's using crutches?

3 Practice the Conversation

Listen to the conversation. Then listen and repeat.

A: What happened to your leg ?

B: I sprained my knee .

A: Did you have to go to the emergency room?

B: Yes, a friend took me there.

A: Did they take an x-ray ?

B: Yes, and then they put this splint on my knee .

Practice the conversation with a partner. Use these ideas.

1	2
hand	leg
cut it	broke it
stitch it up	put you in a wheelchair
put this bandage on it	put this cast on

3	4
elbow	back
sprained it	bruised it
put ice on it	take an x-ray
put this sling on it	gave me this ice pack

All-Star 2 Study Guide

Student Name _____   Date _____

Instructor Name _____

C Put the conversation in order. Number the sentences from first (1) to last (6).

_____ Did you have to go to the emergency room?

_____ Yes, a friend took me.

_____ What happened to your elbow?

_____ Did they put ice on it?

_____ I sprained it.

_____ Yes, and then they gave me this sling.

D Answer the questions about you.

1. When did you have an injury?   _____

2. What kind of injury was it?   _____

3. What body part did you injure?   _____

4. Did you go to the emergency room?   _____

5. What did you do for the injury?   _____

E Read the story. Underline the injury, the body part, and the treatment.

   I sprained my ankle in 2002. I was running down a hill when I slipped.
I went to the emergency room. They took x-rays, but they said I didn't have a
fracture. The doctor put a bandage on my ankle and gave me some crutches.

F Write a story about your injury. Use your answers in Activity D. Follow the model in Activity E.

_____

_____

_____

_____

_____

_____

Recognize sequential order of events in a paragraph. Workbook page 113. LCP-C 49.08

All-Star 2 Study Guide

Student Name _____   Date _____

Instructor Name _____

Follow generic work rules and safety procedures. Interpret safety signs. Workbook page 123.
LCP-C 36.03 . . . CASAS 3.4.2, 4.3.1, 4.3.2, 4.3.4, 4.4.3

C Answer the questions about you.

1. What did you shut off today? _____

2. What did you turn on yesterday? _____

3. What do you usually turn off at night? _____

4. What do you lock? _____

5. What do you unplug when you go away? _____

D Rewrite the polite requests as commands.

1. Would you please unplug the computer?

   _____

2. Could you turn off your cell phone, please?

   _____

3. Would you please lock the door?

   _____

4. Could you please turn down the radio?

   _____

5. Would you take out your books, please?

   _____

E Write a polite request to solve each problem.

1. Your neighbor is playing very loud music.

   _____

2. Your coworker accidentally unplugged the copier.

   _____

All-Star 2 Study Guide for Post-Testing Copyright © McGraw-Hill

All-Star 2 Study Guide

Student Name _____   **Date** _____

Instructor Name _____

See Student Book pages 138–139.

THINGS TO DO

1 Learn New Words 🎧

Look at the pictures. Listen to the words. Then listen and repeat.

① wind   ⑤ snow   ⑨ hurricane
② hail   ⑥ lightning   ⑩ thunderstorm
③ rain   ⑦ sleet   ⑪ tornado
④ fog   ⑧ temperature

Which words are new to you? Circle them.

2 Read and Take Notes

Make a chart like this. Read the emergency procedures. Take notes in the chart.

EMERGENCY	THINGS YOU SHOULD DO	THINGS YOU SHOULDN'T DO
a tornado	go to the basement	stand near a window
a hurricane		
a thunderstorm		

3 Write

Describe an emergency that you or someone you know experienced. Then share your writing with the class.

> EXAMPLE: Several years ago, lightning hit my friend's house. She was home alone at the time. The lightning broke the light over her front door and came into the house through the telephone. No one was hurt but my friend had to buy a new telephone.

★ ★

 TRY THIS Use the Internet to learn more about storms. Find out if there are many hurricanes, thunderstorms, or tornados where you live. If so, find out when the season is for these storms so you can be prepared.

★ ★

Demonstrate understanding of safety/warning signs and emergency procedures. *BEST Plus: Identify government places in the community and describe public services.* Student Book page 138. LCP-C 44.01 . . . CASAS 2.1.2, 2.5.1

BEST *Plus:* I live near the fire station/police station. What about you? Do you live near or far from the fire station/police station?

All-Star 2 Study Guide

Student Name _____ **Date** _____

Instructor Name _____

See Student Book pages 136–137.

Use vocabulary relating to alarm systems (i.e. smoke detectors, fire, house and car alarms). Student Book page 136. LCP-C 44.02 . . . BEST *Plus*

THINGS TO DO

1 Learn New Words 🎧

Look at the picture. Listen to the words. Then listen and repeat.

① smoke   ⑥ attach   ⑪ cover
② spray   ⑦ hydrant   ⑫ ladder
③ fire escape   ⑧ crawl   ⑬ climb up
④ firefighter   ⑨ hose   ⑭ climb down
⑤ fire truck   ⑩ ambulance

Which words are new to you? Circle them.

2 Talk About the Picture

Write 5 things about the picture. Then share your ideas with the class.

EXAMPLE: One firefighter is climbing up the ladder.

3 Put in Order

Put the events in the story in order from first (1) to last (8).

___ He went to bed.

___ He called 911.

___ The smoke alarm in his bedroom went off.

___ The fire trucks arrived.

___ He smelled smoke.

_1_ Sam turned on the electric heater in his bedroom.

___ He woke up.

___ The heater overheated.

4 Read and Write

Read the article on page 137. Use your own ideas to complete the story. Answer these questions in your writing.

1. How did the fire start?
2. Who called 911?
3. Was anyone hurt?
4. How long did it take to put out the fire?

All-Star 2 Study Guide

Student Name _____   Date _____

Instructor Name _____

Describe various weather conditions and appropriate preparation for weather emergencies. Workbook page 128.
LCP-C 47.01 . . . CASAS 2.3.3 . . . BEST *Plus*

A   Look at the picture and the title of the reading. Check the emergency.

❏ flood   ❏ earthquake

❏ hurricane   ❏ tornado

EARTHQUAKE PROCEDURES

An earthquake will usually occur without any type of warning. DO NOT GO OUTSIDE THE BUILDING. Movement of the ground is <u>seldom</u> the actual cause of death or injury. Most injuries result from <u>partial</u> building collapse and falling objects, like <u>toppling</u> chimneys, ceiling plaster, and light fixtures.

During the shaking:

• **IF INDOORS, STAY THERE.** Protect yourself by taking cover under a table, desk, or supported doorway, or crouch against an interior wall. Do not stand under light fixtures, near bookcases, etc. If possible, plan a safe location to take cover in an earthquake.

• Do not leave cover until instructed to do so.

• Do not use elevators.

• **IF OUTDOORS** get into an open area away from trees, buildings, walls, and power lines.

After the shaking:

• Check for injuries.

• Check for fire. Turn off gas.

B   Read the information on earthquake procedures. Circle *should* or *shouldn't*.

EXAMPLE: You (should /(shouldn't)) go outside during an earthquake.

1. You (should / shouldn't) stand near a bookcase.

2. You (should / shouldn't) go under a table.

3. You (should / shouldn't) use elevators.

4. You (should / shouldn't) go under a tree if you are outside.

5. You (should / shouldn't) turn on the gas.

All-Star 2 Study Guide

Student Name _____ **Date** _____

Instructor Name _____

See Workbook page 128.

Describe various weather conditions and appropriate preparation for weather emergencies. Workbook page 129.
LCP-C 47.01 . . . CASAS 2.3.3 . . . BEST *Plus*

C Look at the underlined words in the reading. Match the words and the definitions.

Words	Definitions
1. partial	a. not very often
2. seldom	b. not whole, just part
3. toppling	c. falling

D Circle the correct answer.

1. How can you get hurt in an earthquake?

    A. movement of the ground   B. falling objects

2. Where should you go if you are outside?

    A. under a tree   B. to a open space

3. What should you do if you are inside?

    A. crawl under a desk   B. stand under a light

4. How can you tell if there is going to be an earthquake?

    A. You can't.   B. Pay attention to the warnings.

5. What should you check for after an earthquake?

    A. injuries   B. your wallet

BEST *Plus*: What can people do to prepare for serious weather emergencies like hurricanes, tornadoes, and snow storms?

All-Star 2 Study Guide

Student Name _____ Date _____

Instructor Name _____

WINDOW ON MATH
Converting Temperatures

 Read the information below.

To convert Fahrenheit (F) to Celsius (C), subtract 32, multiply by 5, and divide the result by 9.

> EXAMPLE: It's 50 degrees F. What is the temperature in Celsius? $50 - 32 = 18$; $18 \times 5 = 90$; $90/9 = 10$

To convert Celsius to Fahrenheit, multiply by 9, divide by 5, and add 32.

> EXAMPLE: It's 10 degrees C. What is the temperature in Fahrenheit? $10 \times 9 = 90$; $90/5 = 18$; $18 + 32 = 50$

 Convert these temperatures.

1. 32 °F = _____ °C   3. 40 °C = _____ °F

2. 86 °F = _____ °C   4. 15 °C = _____ °F

Read various temperatures and compare Fahrenheit to Celsius. Student Book page 139. LCP-C 47.02 . . . CASAS 1.1.5, 6.6.4

All-Star 2 Study Guide

Student Name _____   **Date** _____

Instructor Name _____

Describe procedures for basic disposal of trash (regular/large items) and items to be recycled. LCP-C 47.03 . . . CASAS 5.7.1

A Read about trash disposal.

How should we dispose of our trash? There is small trash and large trash. Some small trash we just throw away. Some of our small trash can be used again. It can be recycled. Glass, plastic, and aluminum cans can be recycled. Newspapers can be recycled too. Large trash is put outside for pickup. Old furniture is large trash.

B What should you do with the following items? Put a check in the correct column.

ITEM	THROW AWAY	RECYCLE
1. Diet soda cans		✓
2. Dish washing liquid bottle		
3. Gift wrap paper		
4. Sunday Newspaper		
5. Leftover food		
6. Glass bottles		

C What should you do with hazardous trash such as a car battery? Discuss with a partner.

All-Star 2 Study Guide for Post-Testing Copyright © McGraw-Hill

All-Star 2 Study Guide

Student Name _____   Date _____

Instructor Name _____

See Student Book pages 132–133.

THINGS TO DO

1 Learn New Words 🎧

Look at the pictures. Listen to the words. Then listen and repeat.

① shut off	⑤ turn off	⑧ lock
② plug in	⑥ put back	⑨ unlock
③ take out	⑦ turn down	⑩ unplug
④ turn on		

2 Write

Make a chart like this. Write 3 things you see in each room.

BEDROOM	KITCHEN	LIVING ROOM
a lamp	a refrigerator	

Now use the pictures to tell what Mr. Sanchez did this morning. See page 174 for past tense of irregular verbs.

EXAMPLE: Mr. Sanchez shut off the alarm clock.

3 Practice the Conversation 🎧

Listen to the conversation. Then listen and repeat

A: Could you unplug the heater for me?

B: Sure. Where is it ?

A: It's in the bedroom .

B: Okay. I'll do it right away.

Practice the conversation with a partner. Use these ideas.

1 turn down the heat

the thermostat

in the dining room

2 plug in the fan

it

in the living room

3 lock the front door

the key

on the table

4 💡

Demonstrate knowledge of operating equipment necessary for home and work. Student Book page 132.
LCP-C 38.01 . . . CASAS 4.5.4 . . . BEST *Plus*

All-Star 2 Study Guide

Student Name _____ **Date** _____

Instructor Name _____

Fill out the rental agreement form.

RENTAL APPLICATION

Address of Premises: _____

Description: _____

Rental Start Date: _____	Lease Term (months): _____
Rent (monthly): $ _____	Security Deposit: $ _____
Application Fee: $ _____	# of Occupants: _____

Applicant Information:

Name: _____

Current Address: _____

Home Tel. Number: _____	Work Tel. Number: _____
Driver's License No.: _____	Social Security No.: _____

Applicant's Employment History:

Occupation: _____

Company Name: _____

Employer Tel. Number: _____	Years at this Job: _____
Employer Contact: _____	Years in this field: _____
	Current Salary: $ _____

Applicant's Financial History:

Checking Account #: _____	Savings Account #: _____

Bank Name: _____

Bank Address: _____

Have you ever been evicted? _____

Name of Current Landlord: _____ Tel. Number: _____

CONSENT TO OBTAIN CREDIT INFORMATION

As a material inducement to be considered as a tenant for the Premises, I herewith consent to and authorize _____ , or any agent of same, to contact all references named in this application, and to conduct a credit review, including obtaining my credit report from including obtaining my credit report from any authorized credit reporting agency. I declare under penalty of perjury that the information listed in this application is true and correct. Executed on this _____ day of _____ 2005, in the city of _____ state of _____ .

All-Star 2 Study Guide

Student Name _____   Date _____

Instructor Name _____

See Student Book pages 134–135.

All-Star 2 Study Guide for Post-Testing Copyright © McGraw-Hill

THINGS TO DO

1 Learn New Words 🎧

Look at the pictures. Listen to the words. Then listen and repeat.

① leak	⑦ clothes dryer	⑬ get stuck
② faucet	⑧ hair dryer	⑭ key
③ pipe	⑨ get plugged up	⑮ elevator
④ roof	⑩ sink	⑯ sliding door
⑤ overheat	⑪ toilet	
⑥ space heater	⑫ bathtub	

2 Practice the Conversation 🎧

Listen to the telephone conversation. Then listen and repeat.

A: Hi. This is your tenant in apartment 101.

B: Hi. What can I do for you?

A: Could you please take a look at my refrigerator ?

B: Is the door stuck again?

A: No. This time it's leaking .

B: Okay. I'll be over as soon as I can.

Practice the conversation with a partner. Use these ideas.

1 dryer	**2** sliding door	**3** bathroom sink	**4**
Is it overheating	Is it stuck	Is it leaking	
the door is stuck	I can't lock it	it's plugged up	

3 Write

Choose a problem from Activity 2. Complete the form below.

MAINTENANCE REQUEST FORM

Date:	
Time:	
Name:	
Problem:	
Signature:	

Report housing maintenance, repairs, and problems. *BEST Plus: Describe maintenance problems in the home and how to get them repaired.* Student Book page 134. LCP-C 45.08 . . . CASAS 1.4.7 . . . BEST Plus

BEST *Plus:* When something breaks in your home, who fixes it?

All-Star 2 Study Guide for Post-Testing Copyright © McGraw-Hill

All-Star 2 Study Guide

Student Name _____   Date _____

Instructor Name _____

D Look at the graph. Circle the correct answer below.

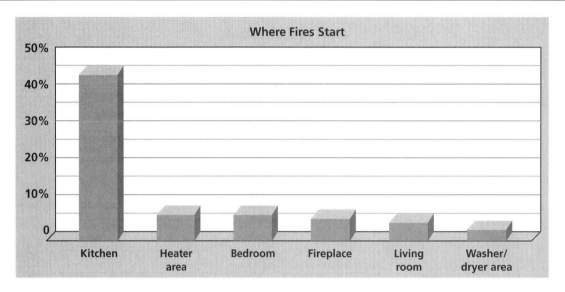

Where Fires Start

1. Where do most fires start in the house?

   A. in the living room   B. in the kitchen

2. Do more fires start near the heater or near the dryer?

   A. near the heater   B. near the dryer

3. What percentage of fires start in the bedroom?

   A. 7%   B. 3%

4. What percentage of fires start in the kitchen?

   A. 45%   B. 4.5%

All-Star 2 Study Guide

Student Name _____   Date _____

Instructor Name _____

Use common verbs, contracted forms, and correct spelling in present tense, present continuous, future (*will, going to,*) past tense, present perfect, modals (present, past). Student Book page 146. LCP-C 50.02 . . . BEST *Plus*

FUTURE WITH *WILL*

Statements		Contractions		
		Affirmative	*Negative*	
I		I'll	I won't	**Tip**
He		he'll	he won't	
She	**will be** there tomorrow.	she'll	she won't	Use *will* to make a
It	**won't be** here tomorrow.	it'll	it won't	promise, to offer
You		you'll	you won't	help, or to make a
We	won't = will not	we'll	we won't	prediction.
They		they'll	they won't	

1 Complete the conversations with *will*, *'ll*, or *won't*.

1. A: Are you going to the party on Saturday?

    B: Yes, I am, but I _____ probably be late.

2. A: Are you going to be home early tonight?

    B: No, I _____ . I have to work until 9:00.

3. A: Did you finish your homework?

    B: No, I didn't. I _____ finish it tomorrow.

4. A: Can we talk about this later?

    B: Sure. I _____ call you tonight.

5. A: Do you think Jean will go to the movies with us?

    B: No, I'm sure she _____ .

6. A: Do you want to get together tomorrow?

    B: No, I can't. I think I _____ be at work all day.

7. A: Is your brother still sick?

    B: Yes, he is, but I think he _____ be better by tomorrow.

8. A: Is it going to rain tomorrow?

    B: I think so, but it _____ rain until the afternoon.

All-Star 2 Study Guide

Student Name _____   **Date** _____

Instructor Name _____

See Student Book pages 148–149.

Read and understand job titles and descriptions. Student Book page 148. LCP-C 35.01 ...CASAS 4.1.3

THINGS TO DO

1 Learn New Words 🎧

Look at the pictures. Listen to the words. Then listen and repeat.

1. computer programmer
2. accountant
3. administrative assistant
4. dental assistant
5. caregiver
6. nursing assistant
7. assembler
8. machine operator
9. painter
10. electrician
11. bricklayer
12. welder

Which words are new to you? Circle them.

2 Write

Choose a job to complete each sentence. More than one answer may be possible.

1. _An accountant_ works with numbers.
2. _____ takes care of sick people.
3. _____ cleans teeth.
4. _____ fixes electrical problems.
5. _____ puts parts together.
6. _____ works with metal.
7. _____ takes phone messages.

3 Find Someone Who

Talk to different classmates. Find someone who answers yes to each question. Write the person's name.

A: Do you want to work in an office ?
B: Yes, I do. (or No, I don't.)

Find someone who_____.	Person's Name
wants to work in an office	_____
likes to work with numbers	_____
wants to work in health care	_____
wants to work outdoors	_____

All-Star 2 Study Guide

Student Name _____ Date _____

Instructor Name _____

See Student Book pages 152–153.

THINGS TO DO

1 Learn New Words 🎧

Look at the pictures. Listen to the words. Then listen and repeat.

① employment office   ⑤ file cabinet   ⑨ day shift
② conference room   ⑥ file folder   ⑩ evening shift
③ supply cabinet   ⑦ full time   ⑪ night shift
④ cubicle   ⑧ part time

Which words are new to you? Circle them.

2 Talk About the Picture

Write 5 things about the picture. Then share your ideas with the class.

EXAMPLE: Mia is very organized.

3 Practice the Conversation 🎧

Listen to the conversation. Then listen and repeat.

A: Do you have any experience as a welder ?
B: Yes, I do. I worked as one in my country.
A: Are you good at working on a team ?
B: Yes, I am. I had to work on a team in my last job.
A: Would you rather work the day shift or the night shift ?
B: I prefer the day shift but I can work either one.

Practice the conversation with a partner. Use these ideas.

1 an accountant/working independently	2 a nursing assistant/solving problems
work independently	solve problems
full time or part time	the evening shift or the night shift
full time	the night shift

3 a machine operator/fixing things quickly	4 a caregiver/following directions
fix things quickly	follow directions
days or evenings	full time or part time
evenings	part time

Recognize and use basic work-related vocabulary. BEST Plus: Demonstrate understanding of basic work-related vocabulary. Student Book page 152. LCP-C 35.02 . . . CASAS 4.1.5, 4.1.6 . . . BEST Plus

BEST *Plus:* Do people usually take breaks at work? How are the jobs of firefighters and police different?

All-Star 2 Study Guide

Student Name _____ **Date** _____

Instructor Name _____

Use various sources to identify job opportunities and inquire about a job (newspapers, agencies). Student Book page 158. LCP-C 35.04 . . . CASAS 4.1.3

1 Read and Identify

Tell about the jobs in the ads. Check (✓) your answers.

	JOB A	JOB B	JOB C	
1.	☐	☐	☐	is in health care.
2.	☐	☐	☐	pays well.
3.	☐	☐	☐	has night shifts available.
4.	☐	☐	☐	requires good people skills.
5.	☐	☐	☐	requires travel.
6.	☐	☐	☐	requires previous experience.

C

Service Technician
Service/repair equipment in textile manufacturing. Strong problem solving skills and electronic background a plus. Travel required. Good benefits and pay. Submit resume: J. Medford, P.O. Box 312, Harrisburg, PA.

A

Nursing Assistants Wanted
Needed for home care. Spanish-speaking CNAs needed for Hispanic cases. All shifts available. Great benefits. Must be punctual and good with people. Call ReLease Nurses at (601) 555-4800.

B

EXPERIENCED CONSTRUCTION WORKERS NEEDED

Painters, carpenters, bricklayers. Good pay. Travel required. Some long hours. Please contact Building Personnel at (336) 555-4670.

All-Star 2 Study Guide for Post-Testing Copyright © McGraw-Hill

All-Star 2 Study Guide

Student Name _____   Date _____

Instructor Name _____

B Circle the correct answer.

1. Can he follow directions well?
   - A. I think so.
   - B. No, he didn't.

2. Is she punctual?
   - A. Yes, she does.
   - B. No, she isn't.

3. Are they dependable?
   - A. Yes, they can.
   - B. No, they aren't.

4. Do you work well with others?
   - A. Yes, I do.
   - B. No, I am not.

5. Does the job require computer skills?
   - A. Yes, it does.
   - B. No, you don't.

C Answer the questions about you. Use *can, can't, do, don't, am, am not, did,* or *didn't.*

1. Do you work well with others?   _____

2. Can you work independently?   _____

3. Are you good at following directions?   _____

4. Are you always punctual?   _____

5. Did you solve problems in your last job?   _____

6. Do you have excellent computer skills?   _____

7. Can you fix electrical problems?   _____

Demonstrate appropriate responses to interview questions, proper behavior, and positive image for job interview. *BEST Plus:* Demonstrate ability to respond to basic interview questions and recognize acceptable standards of behavior during a job interview. Workbook pages 140–141. LCP-C 36.02 . . . CASAS 4.1.5, 4.2.1 . . . BEST Plus

BEST *Plus:* I get nervous at job interviews. What about you?

All-Star 2 Study Guide

Student Name _____   Date _____

Instructor Name _____

Identify the importance of job evaluations for promotions and retention. LCP-C 37.03 . . . CASAS 4.4.2

A Read and complete the chart for yourself.

Your supervisor will evaluate your job performance. It is important to have a good evaluation. If you want a promotion, you must have an excellent evaluation.

	ABOVE AVERAGE	AVERAGE	BELOW AVERAGE
My computer skills are			
My people skills are			
My problem-solving skills are			
My ability to work with others is			
My ability to follow directions is			

B Write about yourself.

My _____ skills are above average.

My ability to _____ is average.

C Think about your job. How will your supervisor rate you? Check *above average*, *average*, or *below average*. Then, answer the questions.

	ABOVE AVERAGE	AVERAGE	BELOW AVERAGE
Are you punctual?			
Can you solve problems?			
Do you work well on a team?			
Can you follow directions?			
Are you dependable?			

Will you get the promotion? _____

Why? _____

_____

All-Star 2 Study Guide

Student Name _____   Date _____

Instructor Name _____

A Read the information on the website. Check the suggestions that are on the website.

Starting a New Job

Starting a New Job

Start off on the right foot

So you're starting a new job soon. Congratulations! Of course you're a little nervous. You can begin right now to make a good start. You need to organize:

- What to wear
- Your transportation
- Childcare, if necessary

What to wear

You need to wear clothes that meet the dress code at work. In some workplaces, you will wear a uniform, in others, you need business attire, and in some you'll wear casual or dress casual clothes.

Uniforms: If your new employer did not tell you where to get your uniform, look up "uniforms" in the telephone book. Call and ask if the store has what you need.

Business/casual attire: Business attire usually means a suit, or a coat and tie for men, and a suit or jacket and dress for women. Of course you can go to a department store for business or casual attire. Thrift shops also carry business clothes at a cheaper price.

Childcare

Childcare

- Get childcare now. Contact your local Child Care Resource Agency.
- Ask other parents for referrals.
- Get medical forms completed and any necessary immunizations.
- Have emergency contact information available.

Transportation

Transportation

- How will you get to work? Make a plan now. Do a practice trip so you know how long it will take.
- Plan for extra time. Make sure you add 15–30 minutes in case there is a problem.
- Have a back-up plan. What if something does go wrong (the car won't start)? You need to have another way to get there.
- Call if you are going to be late.

Suggestions:

- ☐ Be on time.
- ☐ Go to a thrift store for better prices.
- ☐ Call if you are going to be late.
- ☐ Have a back-up plan.
- ☐ Get a bus schedule.

- ☐ Talk to other parents.
- ☐ Fill out medical forms.
- ☐ Look in the telephone book for "uniforms."
- ☐ Plan for extra time.

Identify appropriate behavior, attire, attitudes, and social interactions for promotion. Workbook page 144.
LCP-C 37.04 . . . CASAS 4.4.1, 4.4.2

All-Star 2 Study Guide

Student Name _____   **Date** _____

Instructor Name _____

Read a simple story and utilize context clues for comprehension. Workbook page 148. LCP-C 49.16

B Read the story. Circle the correct answers to the questions below.

Monica Jen got a new job two years ago. She started working for a company that designs and builds new office buildings. Monica was still a student and didn't have much money. She didn't have to wear business attire except to important meetings, but she did need to wear "business casual" clothes. That meant no jeans or T-shirts.

Monica looked up "thrift shops" in the yellow pages of the telephone book. She went to three of the stores and found some very nice used clothing. She bought several outfits for less than $50.

Now Monica has a lot more money for clothes. Some of her clothes are still good but they don't fit anymore. Monica found out about an organization called Dress for Success. This organization gives suits to people who don't have money so they can go to job interviews. Monica gave her suits to Dress for Success.

1. What happened two years ago?

   A. Monica started school.   B. Monica started a new job.

2. What kind of clothes did Monica have to get for work?

   A. suits and business casual clothes   B. T-shirts and jeans

3. Why did she decide to go to thrift shops for clothes?

   A. She didn't have a lot of money.   B. They have new clothes.

4. How did she find information on thrift shops?

   A. She asked Dress for Success.   B. She looked in the yellow pages.

5. Where did she donate her old suits?

   A. Dress for Success   B. a thrift shop

All-Star 2 Study Guide for Post-Testing Copyright © McGraw-Hill

All-Star 2 Study Guide

Student Name _____   Date _____

Instructor Name _____

WINDOW ON PRONUNCIATION 🎧
Intonation in *Yes/No* and *Wh-* Questions

A Listen to the questions. Then listen and repeat.

Rising intonation in *yes/no* questions	Drop-rise intonation in *Wh-* questions
Are you applying for this position?	Why are you applying for this position?
Did you work before?	Where did you work before?
Did you travel?	What did you do?
Did you supervise others?	How many people did you supervise?
Do you have any questions?	What questions do you have?

B Write 3 more questions of each type that an employer might ask in an interview.

Rising intonation in *yes/no* questions	Drop-rise intonation in *Wh-* questions
1.	1.
2.	2.
3.	3.

C Work with a partner. Role play a job interview. Ask and answer the questions.

Use appropriate rhythm and stress in phrases and simple sentences. Student Book page 157. LCP-C 51.05 ... BEST *Plus*

BEST *Plus* Descriptors and Practice Questions

Unit	BEST *Plus* Descriptor	BEST *Plus* Practice Question	Study Guide page
1	Identify self and share personal information. State information about country of origin and current residence.	Where are you from? Where do you live now? How long have you lived in the United States?	1
1	Use appropriate expressions to express feelings and emotions.	Look at the picture on page 9 of the Student Book. How do the people feel?	3
1	Describe self, family members, and others (physical characteristics and personal traits).	Who are the members of your family? Do you have brothers or sisters? Tell me about your family members.	4
1	Communicate impressions, likes, dislikes, and acceptance and rejection to invitations.	What do you like about living in your neighborhood? this country/this city? What housework do you like better, cooking or washing the dishes? What kind of exercise do you like to do? What do you like to do with your family?	8
2	Locate various businesses, and government and community agencies in local area (doctor's office, school, hospital, post office, church).	Where do you go to check out books? Where do you usually study? Where do you go when you need to see a doctor? Where do you go shopping?	13
2	Describe transportation preferences; describe best ways to travel.	Do you take a train or a bus to school? Do you walk? What are some problems you see with transportation in (your city)?	21
3	Identify various methods for making purchases and state a preference.	Do you like to go shopping? How do you pay for your purchases (ATM, credit card, check, cash)? Do you think it is a good idea to use a credit card or ATM card?	28
4	Locate neighborhood school and describe preferences about schools.	Where do children in your area go to school? Do you like the schools in your city/neighborhood?	41
4	Describe reasons why people immigrate and choose to become a U.S. citizen.	Why did you come to this country? Why do people immigrate to another country? Is it important for immigrants to become citizens?	45
5	Communicate impressions, likes, dislikes, acceptance and rejection.	Do you like to go shopping? Where do you like to shop?	56
5	Demonstrate understanding of comparative shopping.	Are clothes or furniture in the United States cheap or expensive? Do you use coupons when you shop?	49
5	Identify articles of clothing, U.S. sizes, quality, and prices.	What do you buy when you go shopping?	52
6	Describe and state opinion about American diet.	What do you think about the American diet? Is American food healthy? Some people think American fruit and vegetables look good but don't taste good: do you agree?	58
6	Describe holidays and customs in one's native country.	Describe your favorite holiday in your country.	59
7	Describe family members and describe family traditions.	Describe someone in your family. What do you usually do to celebrate a holiday?	69
7	Describe preferences about fun and entertainment.	Look at Student Book page 103. What are the people doing? What do you like to do? What do you usually do for fun?	70

Unit	BEST *Plus* Descriptor	BEST *Plus* Practice Question	Study Guide page
8	Describe methods of treating common illnesses or maladies.	Some people think herbal tea is good for a cold. What do you think? What are some things people can do to stay healthy? What foods do you think are good to eat when you're sick? Why?	79
8	Read and interpret information on medicine labels.	Where do you get your medicine? What do you take when you have a headache?	81
9	Identify government places in the community and describe public services.	I live near the fire station/police station. What about you? Do you live near or far from the fire station/police station? What other services in the community are important?	89
9	Describe various weather conditions and appropriate preparation for weather emergencies.	What can people do to prepare for serious weather emergencies, like hurricanes, tornadoes and snow storms?	92
9	Describe maintenance problems in the home and how to get them repaired.	When something breaks in your home, who fixes it?	97
10	Demonstrate understanding of basic work-related vocabulary.	Do people usually take breaks at work? How are the jobs of firefighters and police different?	101
10	Demonstrate ability to respond to basic interview questions and recognize acceptable standards of behavior during a job interview.	I get nervous at job interviews. What about you?	103